W9-AHA-895

Small Group GUIDE

3

myView

LITERACY

with contributions from:
Dr. Frank Serafini, Dr. Sharon Vaughn, Dr. Jim Cummins,
Dr. Pat Cunningham, Dr. Judy Wallis, Dr. Ernest Morrell

 **Pearson**

Glenview, Illinois   Boston, Massachusetts
Chandler, Arizona   New York, New York

17 Steve Debenport/Getty Images; 22 Hero Images/Getty Images; 46 (BL) Eurobanks/Shutterstock, (BR) Cindy Greene, (TL) Cindy Greene, (TR) Cindy Greene; 47 (BC) Cindy Greene, (BL) Cindy Greene, (TL) Cindy Greene, (TR) Cindy Greene; 48 (BL) SNEHI/Shutterstock, (TL) Cindy Greene, (TR) Cindy Greene; 49 (CL) Cindy Greene, (CR) Cindy Greene, (TL) Cindy Greene, (TR) Cindy Greene.

Pearson Education, Inc. 330 Hudson Street, New York, NY 10013

© Pearson Education, Inc. or its affiliates. All Rights Reserved. Printed in the United States of America.

This publication is protected by copyright, and permission should be obtained from the publisher prior to any prohibited reproduction, storage in a retrieval system, or transmission in any form or by any means, electronic, mechanical, photocopying, recording, or otherwise. [The publisher hereby grants permission to reproduce pages, in part or in whole, for classroom use only, the number not to exceed the number of students in each class. Notice of copyright must appear on all copies.] For information regarding permissions, request forms and the appropriate contacts within the Pearson Education Global Rights & Permissions Department, please visit www.pearsoned.com/permissions/.

PEARSON and ALWAYS LEARNING are exclusive trademarks owned by Pearson Education, Inc. or its affiliates in the US and/or other countries.

Unless otherwise indicated herein, any third party trademarks that may appear in this work are the property of their respective owners and any references to third party trademarks, logos or other trade dress are for demonstrative or descriptive purposes only. Such references are not intended to imply any sponsorship, endorsement, authorization, or promotion of Pearson's products by the owners of such marks, or any relationship between the owner and Pearson Education, Inc. or its affiliates, authors, licensees or distributors.

ISBN-13: 978-0-134-90478-8
ISBN-10:   0-134-90478-8

4 19

Small Group GUIDE

Table of Contents

Introduction

Let's begin with the big question. *How can this guide help you to be more successful in planning, forming, and managing small groups while also making certain all students are engaged in meaningful work?* Whew! It is the goal of this guide to answer that question, and we'll try to answer many other questions along the way.

We'll enlist the help of master teachers, researchers, teacher educators, and curriculum designers to provide you with foundational research as well as practical ideas to try tomorrow. You can use this handbook as reference throughout the year.

Each chapter in the guide is divided into three sections. Each section serves a different purpose, but they work together to support your grouping decisions.

The Big Picture	Setting the Scene	Dig In!
• Learn from *myView* authors and understand the research and pedagogical foundation for the concepts of the chapter • Discover some common misconceptions and possible pitfalls	• Hear from classroom teachers who are dealing with the challenges of meeting students' individual needs while managing a whole class daily • Learn from experienced veterans and novice teachers, too	• Get right into the details and steps of forming, conducting, and managing your instruction • Find anchor charts, management tips, time-saving tricks, and teaching ideas to try on for size

Your journey begins in a place that is your own.

For the Expert	Perhaps you've been running needs-based small groups successfully for a long time and are just looking for some new ideas. You may want to look for some new routines or anchor charts. You may also find some background information to help you as you mentor a new teacher to your team.
For the Proficient	Maybe you feel that managing small groups is a real challenge while keeping the rest of the class engaged in productive work. You may want to get some new management tips. The ideas for independent and student-led group work may be really useful, too.
For the Novice	You might be new to flexibly grouping students into needs-based groups and may be looking for a deeper understanding of why this approach may be helpful for students. The information you will receive is based on the most current research. Knowing how to identify the skills students need to work on is also important. We'll show you how the *myView* program provides tools to assist you. The chapter on forming and organizing groups may give you some more confidence as you move forward.

Point of View
Who's telling this story?

First Person: I am!	Third Person: She is!
Look for these pronouns: I, me, my	Look for these pronouns: She, he, her, him
The speaker or narrator is inside the story.	The speaker or narrator is outside the story.

No matter where your journey begins, we will provide you with support along the way.
Let's get started!

Small Groups in *myView*

Questions Addressed in This Chapter

- Why are small groups important?
- What do small groups look like in a workshop model?
- How do students benefit from small group work?
- What are some of the different types of groups?
- What support does *myView* provide for small groups?

What's new about small groups?

by Frank Serafini, Ph.D. Professor of Literacy Education and Children's Literature, Arizona State University and Jim Cummins (ELL), Ph.D. Professor Emeritus, University of Toronto

How are small groups in a workshop model different from small groups in the past?

Small groups were once thought to be permanent. A student in the Bluebird Group, for example, remained there for the duration of the year. Once assessments were conducted, groups were created based on reading or simply decoding abilities and these groups worked together for the entire year, with little chance of moving out of the "low" group into a higher group. In a workshop model, more fine-grained, ongoing assessments allow teachers to move students in and out of small groups to focus instruction on specific needs when dealing with specific texts. This type of mobility allows students to receive tailored instruction based on specific skills. Small groups serve a variety of purposes and readers' needs and abilities. Small groups come together for limited periods of time as teachers work with readers on strategies and reading skills they need at that particular moment, with that particular text.

How are small groups advantageous to English language learners?

Small groups provide opportunities for teachers to differentiate instruction to meet the comprehension needs of students who are in the process of learning English. Some English language learners have acquired relatively fluent conversational skills in the language and have progressed to Intermediate or Advanced levels. These students still require instructional support to understand the academic language of textbooks and to produce oral and written language that expresses and elaborates on their understanding. Beginners obviously need support for the development of both conversational and academic skills in English.

What are the most common misconceptions about small groups?

One of the most common misconceptions is that small group instruction should only focus on guided reading. Although small groups are often a forum for guided reading, other forms of instruction should also be implemented. Small group instruction can focus on comprehension strategies, writing revisions, literature study discussions, inquiry projects, and other instructional purposes based on the needs of the students.

Another misconception about small group instruction is that all students must meet in a small group situation each and every day. These groups are needs based and should be organized to meet the demands of the students. Therefore, some students may require more or less small group instruction compared to

> " These groups are needs based and should be organized to meet the demands of the students. "

others. Teachers should assess students' needs based on the instructional focus for small group instruction during a workshop and organize students accordingly. For students who are not in small groups, student-led independent and collaborative time is equally important for them to learn to manage their time and learn without the ongoing guidance from a teacher. In light of this, teachers should not feel pressured to meet daily with every student for small group instruction. In order for small group time to be meaningful, it has to be grounded in purpose.

How are small groups different in a balanced literacy or workshop classroom?

As Ms. Luz Rodriguez recounts, "I worked with small groups and the groups would rotate around to my 'teacher station' each day. The students didn't change groups very often. I thought about what each group needed, but now I try to think more about what each student needs." Ms. Rodriguez, now a teacher in Midland, thinks that having students work in flexible, needs-based groups helps her focus on "right-now needs" with her students. Those needs change over time. When students see the relevance of the instruction, engagement increases.

"I'm not the only resource for learning. When students see themselves as part of a small team that is trying to work through the same issues, skills, or texts, they seem more likely to ask help from, or offer help to, other students. When students can teach others, they learn themselves."

Ms. Rodriguez made some changes. Her students now spend a great deal more time working independently while she calls other students over for individual conferencing or to work with a few students on the same skill. They also have ongoing, collaborative projects.

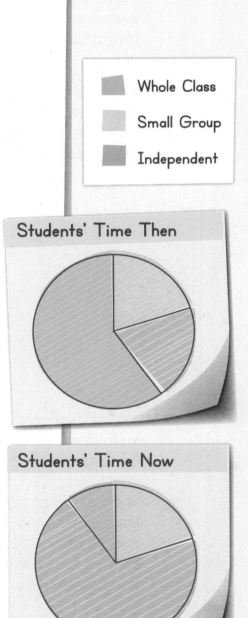

Whole Class

Small Group

Independent

Students' Time Then

Students' Time Now

What changes or shifts can I make in my group instruction?

Change or Shift		I'm Making This Change Because ...
My students will spend more time working independently and less time working as part of a whole group.	→	I want my students to spend more time actually reading and writing.
I will reassess my groups more frequently and make more frequent adjustments.	→	I want students to have "as needed" instruction that they can apply quickly. I want every student to have a chance to advance.
I will confer with individual students more often.	→	I want to assess their individual needs, concerns, and strengths. I want them to become more invested in what they are learning and why.
Some students may work in more than one small group in a day.	→	I want students to be in groups working on skills and strategies that they need right now. If that means a student is part of two different groups on some days, that's fine.
I will encourage students to count on each other and go to each other for help.	→	I want students to see that they are members of a community of learners. Students may have a fresh way of explaining a skill that makes a breakthrough.

What are the benefits of small group instruction?

Research shows that small group instruction helps students acquire and master skills, but just teaching students to read and write isn't enough. There aren't many jobs that adults do in isolation. Most jobs involve working with others, conferring, sharing information, and helping the team be successful. Raising the next generation of citizens who can gather and interpret information, speak effectively, and listen to others is a key goal of education. Students learn these skills in the classroom while working with others. The teacher models and sets up situations for students to develop these skills. The opportunities for social-emotional development while working with others are plentiful.

How do small groups help develop **speaking and listening skills?**

Speaking in front of the whole class may feel very intimidating for some students, and a small group may provide that intermediate step between partner conversations and a larger group. Students need practice speaking about what they know, having their ideas heard, and actively listening to others. Small group settings can provide a safe space for developing these skills. As the teacher, it is important to explicitly teach strategies to help students grow as speakers and listeners.

Rules for Classroom Conversations

Be respectful!
Listen carefully.
Speak when it's your turn.
Look at others when you speak.
Speak clearly.
Stay on the topic.
Ask and answer questions.

Benefits

• Time for explicit instruction and practice
• Close modeling and monitoring of progress
• Less intimidation for reluctant speakers
• Fewer distractions for listening practice

How do small groups help develop **foundational, word-level skills?**

Students may have gaps in their abilities to decode and read some individual words. As you confer with children and closely listen as they read, you'll note these gaps. You can pull aside a few children with similar needs to provide a quick, prescriptive lesson that targets the gaps using text at the students' level.

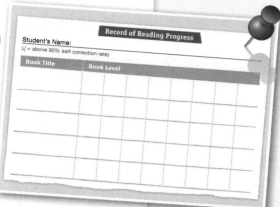

Benefits

- Point-of-need instruction
- Fill gaps for individuals
- Immediate application
- Fast and focused

How do small groups help develop **accuracy and fluency?**

A student who reads fluently and with appropriate expression is more likely comprehending what is being read. Listening to a student read provides a window into their skills of decoding, putting words together into phrases, understanding punctuation, and using intonation. Small group time gives you a chance to model reading short passages and to focus on different aspects of fluency. You can listen to individuals and record their growth toward becoming fluent, independent readers.

Benefits

- Provide opportunities for recording of students' reading progress
- Close monitoring of reading passages
- Point-of-need modeling and support for individual readers
- Explicit instruction of fluency strategies

How do small groups help develop **reading comprehension skills?**

Reading with comprehension is certainly the major goal of reading instruction, but it involves many different elements. For each comprehension skill there are a variety of subskills and strategies that students can use to master that skill. Effective small groups allow you to focus on explicit instruction of strategies with the students who will benefit from them. Students can then practice and internalize these strategies with appropriately-leveled text.

Benefits

- Utilize a more "surgical" rather than "one-size-fits-all" approach
- Enable students to practice the strategies with texts that fit them
- Provide immediate feedback for teachers and learners
- Assess more accurately

Point of View

Who's telling this story?

First Person: I am!	Third Person: She is!
Look for these pronouns: I, me, my	Look for these pronouns: she, he, her, him
The speaker or narrator is inside the story.	The speaker or narrator is outside the story.

Using Text Features

Use text features to find information.

Look for:

➡ Words in Bold Print: Food and water are **needs**.

➡ Words in Italics: The word *want* means "something you wish for."

➡ Key Words About the Topic: People can spend or save for a want.

That's an Exaggeration!

Hyperbole is an exaggerated statement.

I'm really tired.
I'm so tired, I could sleep for a year.

Sam is hungry.
Sam is so hungry, he could eat a horse.

The store has a lot of toys.
The store has millions of toys.

How do small groups help develop skills to read **complex text?**

Challenging, complex texts can offer some wonderful teaching opportunities. Advanced sentence and text structures, challenging vocabulary, multiple text features, and deeper levels of meaning provide a wealth of examples for practicing strategies in context. Students can easily see that the strategies you are sharing with them will be immediately useful in working through their text.

When working with other students in Book Clubs or other collaborative reading situations, students come to see their fellow students as resources. They even realize that they themselves can provide support for other readers.

Benefits

- Provide opportunities to apply strategies immediately
- Build a community of supportive readers
- Focus on more complex strategies and skills
- Use more complex texts to apply previously-taught skills

What are some of the different types of groups?

Students may work independently, as part of a whole class, or in small groups led by the teacher or by the students themselves. Each setting for learning has a purpose. Varying the groupings throughout the day gives students a chance to work and reflect alone, receive instruction from the teacher, and engage in purposeful conversations with others.

As you develop plans for your classroom day, think about how you will provide opportunities for students to work alone, with a partner, as part of a student-led small group, with a teacher in a focused small group setting, and as part of a whole class learning community.

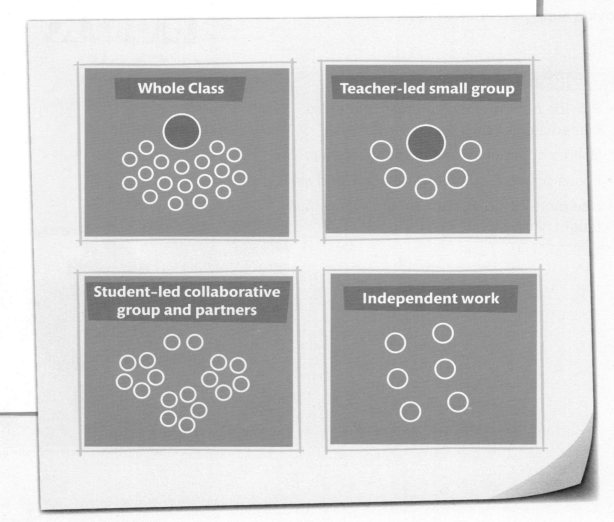

Whole Class Work

In a balanced literacy classroom, there may be less time to spend in whole class instruction than in a more traditional approach, but that whole class time is still important. Maximize the time with careful planning. Prepare the visuals you want to use to introduce new concepts or skills. Practice how you will model reading with expression as you read aloud from a challenging text. Determine how you will pose questions to encourage as many students as possible to participate. Allow time to celebrate the completion of projects so every student feels a sense of accomplishment and accountability.

Effective Uses for Whole Class Work

- Introduce new material
- Review the plans and schedules for the day
- Read aloud a challenging text
- Shared reading and shared writing
- Lead into partner or small group discussions
- Allow students to share and shine after a project

Benefits of Whole Class Work

- Creates a cohesive classroom community
- Establishes a common foundation
- Models and demonstrates skills
- May help auditory learners feel more comfortable

Teacher-Led Small Groups

These groups change and shift depending on diagnosed needs. The teacher makes the lessons relevant to what students are reading and writing. The instruction follows a predicable structure and teaches strategies explicitly. During small group time, the teacher is often conferring with individuals to check for understanding. Members of the group may offer help to others as they proceed toward mastery.

If a student can confidently apply the skill or concept after the initial instruction with the group, that student might work independently for a day or two while the teacher works with others in the group who need more support. Groups are based on assessed needs and are constantly being formed and reformed.

Effective Uses for Teacher-Led Small Groups

- Strategy instruction
- Shared reading and shared writing
- Support and scaffold new learnings
- Quick practice and assessment
- Clarify goals for independent work

Benefits of Teacher-Led Small Groups

- Students see the relevance of each strategy
- Students support each other
- More focused attention from the teacher
- More time spent applying the skill
- More time spent actually reading and writing

Process for Effective Small Groups

While all teachers have individual styles or processes, there are some common steps in planning for and conducting effective small groups. Basing the groups on demonstrated needs keeps them focused and flexible. This type of "right now" instruction keeps the lessons relevant for learners.

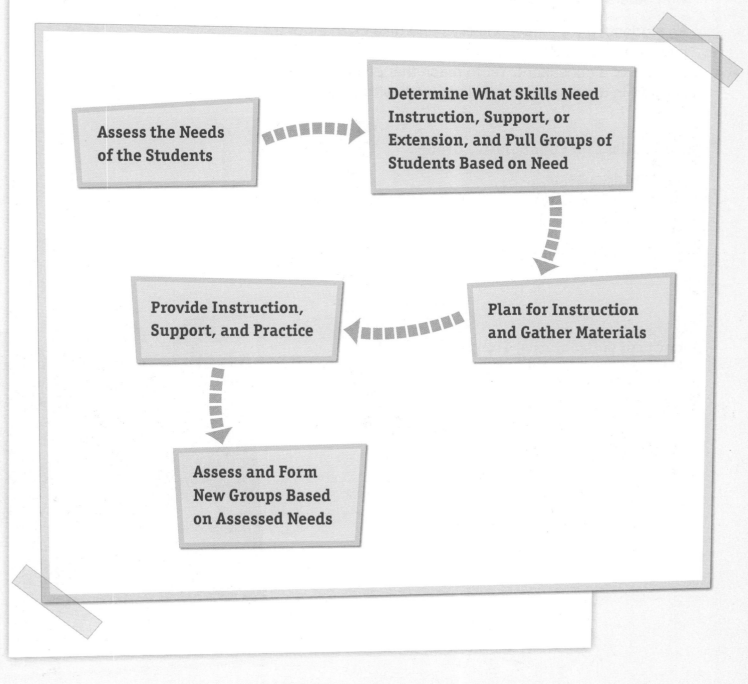

Student-Led Collaborative Groups and Partners

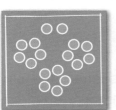

Students may gain confidence working with a partner and then carry that confidence into larger collaborative groups. Taking turns leading and following will help students prepare for working with others throughout their lifetimes.

As students grow in responsibility and take on more of the planning and scheduling of their work, the teacher's role shifts to more of a consultant. Yet to reach that point, students need support in developing the skills to work with others.

Effective Uses for Collaborative Groups

- Partner discussion
- Long-term projects
- Book clubs
- Interest-area reading and research

Benefits of Collaborative Groups

- Practice listening and speaking skills
- Develop planning skills and responsibility
- Support others as a member of a community of learners
- Value diverse learning styles and opinions

Independent Work

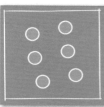

Students need to spend large amounts of time reading, writing, and reflecting. The independent work students do will often be based on goals developed in the small group or in individual conferences with the teacher. During independent work students practice and apply what they have learned and reflect on areas where they need additional support.

Effective Uses for Independent Work

- Practicing and applying strategies
- Following up on small group tasks
- Preparing for Book Club or other group tasks
- Writing assignments
- Independent reading

Benefits of Independent Work

- Build self-reliance
- Assess reading and writing development
- More time spent reading and writing
- Time to reflect

Name _Nessa_

Monday	Begin new story. Look up new vocabulary words.	Write outline.
Tuesday	Work with Lin on first draft of skit. Read chapter 2.	Put anchor chart in strategy notebook.
Wednesday		

How does *myView* support my grouping choices?

The *myView* program provides support for a variety of grouping choices.

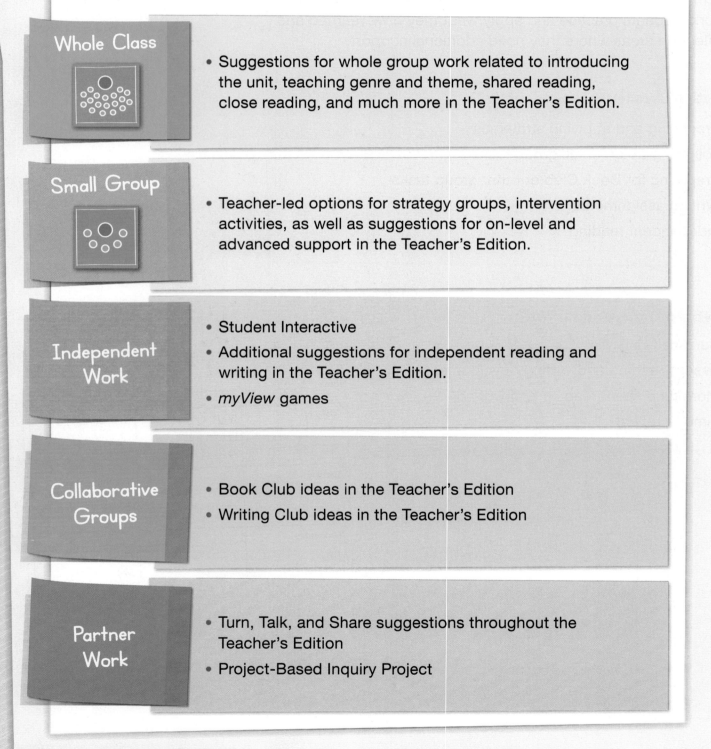

Whole Class

- Suggestions for whole group work related to introducing the unit, teaching genre and theme, shared reading, close reading, and much more in the Teacher's Edition.

Small Group

- Teacher-led options for strategy groups, intervention activities, as well as suggestions for on-level and advanced support in the Teacher's Edition.

Independent Work

- Student Interactive
- Additional suggestions for independent reading and writing in the Teacher's Edition.
- *myView* games

Collaborative Groups

- Book Club ideas in the Teacher's Edition
- Writing Club ideas in the Teacher's Edition

Partner Work

- Turn, Talk, and Share suggestions throughout the Teacher's Edition
- Project-Based Inquiry Project

Chapter 2

Forming and Organizing Groups

Questions Addressed in This Chapter

- How do I decide what to teach and to whom?
- How does assessment inform small group instruction?
- When should students move to a different group?
- How does *myView* help me collect and analyze assessment data?
- How do I use the assessment data in *myView* to form small groups?

How does assessment inform instruction?

What does it mean to group students purposefully?

by Sharon Vaughn, Ph.D. Professor, Department of Special Education, The University of Texas at Austin and Jim Cummins (ELL), Ph.D. Professor Emeritus, University of Toronto

For independent groups, we purposively consider grouping students in terms of their knowledge and skills as well as what role they will serve in the group. For example, independent groups are typically heterogeneous (i.e., mixed ability), meaning that students in the group include those who are above expectations, meeting expectations, and acquiring expectations. This allows students to both extend their learning and to support each other.

Teacher-directed groups are purposively set up to assure proficiency in skills and literacy goals for a select group of students. These groups are established based on students' needs, allowing teachers to specifically guide the instruction to maximize learning.

With students at different levels of English proficiency, how can I improve the accuracy of assessment?

Classroom-based and formative assessment uses a variety of evidence to evaluate each student's achievement of curriculum expectations and can be used to report progress to students, parents, school districts, and the general public. Assessment of learning can draw on a variety of evidence such as formal tests, portfolios, oral reports or presentations, journals, etc.

What are the most common misconceptions about how teachers use assessment to form groups?

One common misunderstanding teachers may have is how to effectively integrate formal, informal, and observational data about students' literacy progress. Effective teachers use all these approaches to make decisions about instruction and to assure that students at all reading levels are meeting benchmarks. Students' scores on school-recommended screening measures or tests and assessments from the previous year need not be the primary information for assigning students to groups. Students may have literacy needs that require more explicit instruction in particular areas, e.g., spelling and writing, that may have not been assessed through the more formal measures. Another common misconception is that assessments are used for forming instructional groups and not used to monitor instruction. This is an important misconception about the role of assessment. Ongoing monitoring of students' responses to instruction is an important mechanism for assessing their growth and needs and reforming groups.

How often should I reevaluate if a student is in the right group?

Groups are adjusted on an ongoing basis to respond to students' learning needs. For example, in independent groups, teachers may adjust these groups every two weeks to provide students with adequate time to have the groups function cooperatively but also not too much time so that they tire of working with the same students. Teacher-led groups can vary considerably, from groups that are relatively stable (i.e., 8 weeks) to groups that are reformed frequently. For example, teachers may have students in relatively stable groups for their group literacy instruction but may pull subgroups of students for specific types of instruction, e.g., practicing reading and writing vowel teams. Teachers use ongoing progress monitoring data to facilitate decision making.

How can I gather and use information efficiently to plan for my small group time?

Gathering data, without using that information to adjust instruction, doesn't help students become more proficient. By identifying a student's strengths, you can use them to build on new skills. Identifying a challenging area will help you know what gaps you may need to fill.

A grade-level team got together with the school's reading specialist to discuss collecting and using information. Each teacher brought a tip to share. They discussed how they would use the information to inform their instruction.

Collecting Information

- Keep an online or paper clipboard with you for jotting down observations.
- Always begin a conference with a specific compliment about something the student has done.

- Chart commonly missed items. Look for students with similar needs.
- Each test item aligns with a skill or standard. You may use that information for small group instruction that targets those areas.

Observation and Conferring

Formal Assessments

Samples of Student Work

Informal Progress Checks

- Take digital photos of student work as part of a digital portfolio or send the photos in a brag email to the family.
- Have a "Select a Sample" time before conferring. Ask students to choose one sample that shows that they were very successful and one sample that was very challenging for them.

- Have students hold up one to five fingers to show how confident they are that they understood the new skill.
- Ask students to turn to a partner and explain the key point of the lesson. Have students shake hands if they have the same understanding.

Using Information

Observations and Conferring

"The most valuable information I get is from watching and listening to my students." Students feel more ownership over their learning when they confer with the teacher and agree on the next goals and tasks. They see the purpose in what they are learning and how it will help them.

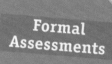

Formal Assessments

"Tests help me pick up on a gap I might not have noticed. I try to recheck to see if the item confused the student or if the skill was not mastered." Create a similar version of a missed test item and work through it together with the student when conferring to identify a strategy that might be helpful.

Samples of Student Work

"I ask my students to explain how work collected earlier in the year differs from the work they do now. This helps me see if they can verbalize the skills and strategies they used." You might ask students to go back to a saved work sample and see how they might adjust it based on their new skills.

Informal Progress Checks

"I usually do a quick check a couple of minutes before I need to end the lesson to give myself time to rephrase anything that was misunderstood. I love to compliment the group for what they learned." It is good to jot down any misunderstandings or concerns to use as a springboard when you begin the lesson the next day.

What should I listen or watch for when I observe students?

Good teachers are always doing detective work. They are on the lookout for clues to what students need. Keeping track of the observations and conferring notes translates that detective work into point-of-need instruction.

When I ask...	I see and hear...	It may mean...
How does this help you as a reader or writer?	[eye contact] "I can use it to understand why the character acted that way based on the feeling words I read."	The student can provide a cause-and-effect relationship to the skill and its use. He or she got it!
	[no eye contact] "It helps me read better."	A vague answer may mean the student is not confident in the skill or strategy. Try conferring to learn more.
How would you help younger students get better at this skill?	[reaches for example text] "I'd start by showing them the pictures and then I'd have them draw the place. We'd talk about why the setting matters. Then we'd read on to see if the setting changes."	Several strategies are provided and it is evident that the purpose of the skill is clear. He or she got it!
	"I'd show them the chart."	The student may not have internalized the skill and is using the strategy anchor chart as a crutch. Perhaps reteach with a new strategy and a less complex text.

What can I learn from formal assessments and what can I not learn?

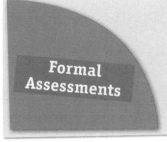
Formal Assessments

Formal assessments may involve a high-stakes standardized or state-mandated test or just a test you give each week that helps you create grades for report cards. Each type of test has a purpose, but it's important to also understand the limitations of each type of testing.

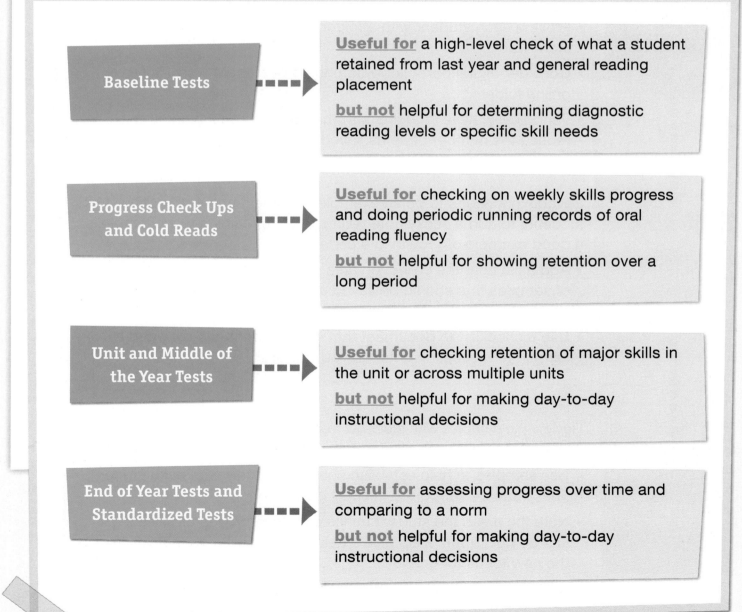

Baseline Tests ➔ <u>Useful for</u> a high-level check of what a student retained from last year and general reading placement

<u>but not</u> helpful for determining diagnostic reading levels or specific skill needs

Progress Check Ups and Cold Reads ➔ <u>Useful for</u> checking on weekly skills progress and doing periodic running records of oral reading fluency

<u>but not</u> helpful for showing retention over a long period

Unit and Middle of the Year Tests ➔ <u>Useful for</u> checking retention of major skills in the unit or across multiple units

<u>but not</u> helpful for making day-to-day instructional decisions

End of Year Tests and Standardized Tests ➔ <u>Useful for</u> assessing progress over time and comparing to a norm

<u>but not</u> helpful for making day-to-day instructional decisions

How can I better manage, document, and interpret student progress using work samples?

Samples of Student Work

Manage

Students generate a lot of work samples, and keeping your classroom from becoming a cluttered version of a proud family's refrigerator door takes planning. Each student needs to know what work should be saved and where it should be placed.

- Provide each student with a folder, box, or large envelope to store work.
- Consider digital portfolios with photos of student work stored in online folders.
- Periodically, have students sort through their past work and reduce the number of items saved.

Document

Saved work needs to be an example of something worth noting. Ask students to add a sticky note telling why they think a work sample is a good example of growth in a certain area.

- Add a list near the collection area to remind students of the types of samples that should be saved and the due dates. Have students add a checkmark when they have saved samples.
- Use a checklist to document that each student has provided a sample to meet each criterion you establish.

Interpret

Review the samples with students frequently. Ask why they saved each item and the skills each shows. Ask what was easy or challenging.

- Use samples to help establish needs and goals with each student. These can be supported in small group work.
- Note the areas the student thinks can be improved or skills that can be built upon. Help give a name to the skill area that will be the new focus for growth.
- Begin and end these sample review sessions with a compliment.

How can I quickly check in with students to see if they understood the skill?

When teaching a lesson, it is important to be frequently checking with students to see if they are misunderstanding or are grasping the concepts. Frequent questioning avoids students getting more confused as the lesson continues. Having students demonstrate quickly what they learned helps you plan the next steps for the group or individuals.

RESTATEMENT
Ask students to put into their own words what you have explained. Check for confusion or misinterpretation.

PROMPTS
Ask: How might you use this? What was the most important thing you learned? How does this connect to our last lesson?

VISUAL CHECKS
Have students use signals such as thumbs up or down or yes/no card to provide quick feedback to a question.

QUICK CHECKS
Use the Quick Checks in *myView* and the if/then suggestions to differentiate small group work.

LESSON SUMMARIES
Have students jot down answers to a question or two to review the lesson. What three things did you learn? When will you use this skill? What is still somewhat unclear?

REFLECTIONS
Encourage students to reflect on what they learned in the lesson, how it will help them, and what was easy or challenging.

How can I make the time I spend conferring with students more purposeful?

Conferring with individual students weekly helps inform your instruction, check on your students' progress, and gives you an opportunity to provide feedback as students work. Conferring is most effective when there is a clear purpose and structure.

- Establish the focus. What specific skill or area are you discussing or checking?
- Plan how you will record information. Will you use a checklist or other prepared form? Will you use a conferring notebook?
- Prepare your materials. Do you need leveled text, work samples, running record sheets, or anchor charts?

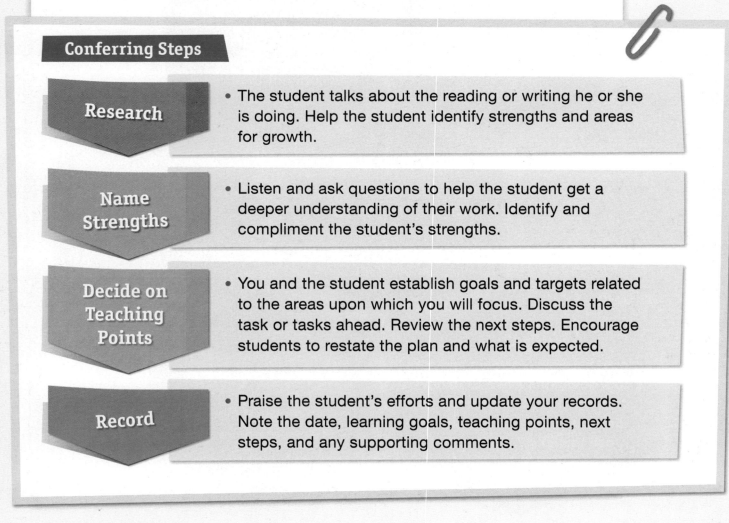

Conferring Steps

Research
- The student talks about the reading or writing he or she is doing. Help the student identify strengths and areas for growth.

Name Strengths
- Listen and ask questions to help the student get a deeper understanding of their work. Identify and compliment the student's strengths.

Decide on Teaching Points
- You and the student establish goals and targets related to the areas upon which you will focus. Discuss the task or tasks ahead. Review the next steps. Encourage students to restate the plan and what is expected.

Record
- Praise the student's efforts and update your records. Note the date, learning goals, teaching points, next steps, and any supporting comments.

Conferring Recoding Sheet

Student's Name

Date

Text being shared:

STUDENT'S COMMENTS

Insights or learnings:

Struggles and strengths:

TEACHER/STUDENT DISCUSSION NOTES

Instructional focus:

GOALS AND NEXT STEPS

Focus area:

Task(s):

Student's Name

Date

Text being shared:

STUDENT'S COMMENTS

Insights or learnings:

Struggles and strengths:

TEACHER/STUDENT DISCUSSION NOTES

Instructional focus:

GOALS AND NEXT STEPS

Focus area:

Task(s):

What are some ways to better manage record keeping as I assess and learn more about what each student needs?

Using recording sheets can help you avoid jotting notes on little scraps of paper that you then spend time transferring to another location. Select recording sheets that best match your needs and record the results digitally or keep the recording sheets together in a binder or on a clipboard that you keep handy.

Student's Name:	Date:
Student's Strengths and Skills to Build Upon:	New Skills to Target:
Student's Name:	Date:
Student's Strengths and Skills to Build Upon:	New Skills to Target:

Reading Record

Students' Names	Book Title and Level	Observations

Record of Reading Progress

Student's Name: _____

($\sqrt{}$ = above 90% self-correction rate)

Book Title	Book Level								

Record of Conferences

Students' Names	Dates of Conferences and Level of Text Covered			

How does *myView* help me effectively use assessment to inform my small group decisions?

The *myView* program provides many assessment options. These assessments can be found in print and are also available online on PearsonRealize.com. Choose the assessments that will be most beneficial for the needs in your classroom.

Baseline Test
- Given at the beginning of the year to gather a foundation of information
- Provides a snapshot of a student's abilities

Progress Check-Ups
- Assesses skills taught that week
- Monitors progress to intervene as needed

Cold Reads
- New passages that can be used as needed to check comprehension and check comprehension skill practice
- Can be used for a fluency check using running records

Weekly Standards Practice
- Given at the end of a lesson as an "exit ticket" to check students' knowledge of specific literacy skills

Unit Tests
- Assesses the key skills from each week's instruction in the unit

Middle-of-Year Test
- Monitors student progress on skills and standards taught in Units 1–3

End-of-Year Test
- Gives a summative view of a student's progress for the year

Assessment Guide
- Provides professional development and printables to support observational assessment and progress monitoring

Chapter 3

Managing Small Groups

Questions Addressed in This Chapter

- How do small groups fit into my day?
- What should I consider when planning for small groups?
- How can I set up my classroom to effectively manage small groups?
- What steps will help me manage my small group time?
- How can I help the transitions between groups go smoothly?
- How does *myView* help me plan for small groups?

What should I consider when I plan for small groups?

by Dr. Pat Cunningham, Ph.D. Professor, Wake Forest University

How can I help students make smoother transitions between activities?

Transitions are always difficult, but you must teach children to transition quickly if you are going to have enough time to work with small groups. The most efficient teachers make sure that students know when their group will convene and have a signal (hand clap or short song) they use to signal students that it is time. Many teachers use this transition time as a "brain break" and encourage the kids to "dance" to where they are going as a one-minute song plays. Students all try to be in their new spot when the music stops.

How can I help students track their own work and learn to manage their time better?

Students will focus on their independent work if they have a short, consistent period of time to do it and if they consider it worthwhile. Students who are reading books of their own choosing or working on computer games that teach reading skills or working on a project with their book club group will be engaged and make every minute count. If they are completing worksheets or other assignments that have no intrinsic value for them, they will dawdle and be easily distracted.

What elements of a small group lesson should I plan most carefully?

Small group reading lessons should always focus students' attention on a particular comprehension skill or strategy. Teachers who make the best use of their small group time teach and model the comprehension skill or strategy with the whole class. The purpose of a small group is to have students apply that skill or strategy to text at their level. Major planning is required for the whole class lesson. The teacher coaches students to figure out words and word meanings as well as to focus on the comprehension skill.

> " The purpose of a small group is to have students apply that skill or strategy to text at their level. "

What is a common challenge for teachers planning for, and managing, small groups?

The biggest challenge for teachers at all grade levels is being able to meaningfully occupy the students not in the teacher-led group. Often students are expected to work independently at their seats or in centers. Having students read independently or work on reading skills with partners or on computers allows them to make good use of the time when they are not with the teacher.

Setting the Scene

How can I set up my classroom to more effectively manage my small groups?

There are infinite ways to arrange a classroom. When thinking about small group instruction, consider the placement of a table for small group work and access to materials that will be needed. The picture below of Mr. Para's class shows some of his considerations for the small group area.

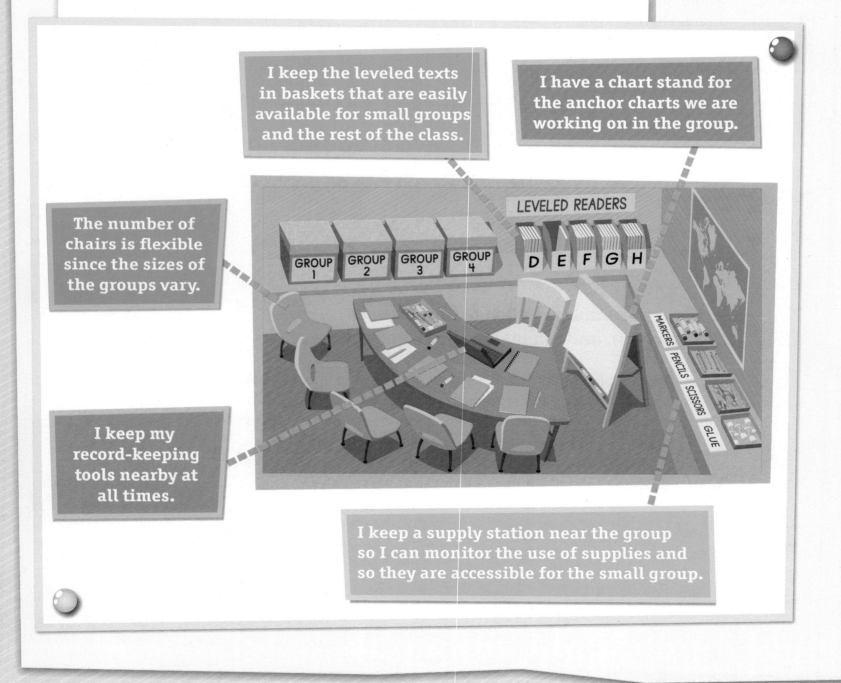

I keep the leveled texts in baskets that are easily available for small groups and the rest of the class.

I have a chart stand for the anchor charts we are working on in the group.

The number of chairs is flexible since the sizes of the groups vary.

I keep my record-keeping tools nearby at all times.

I keep a supply station near the group so I can monitor the use of supplies and so they are accessible for the small group.

What physical elements in the classroom can help in managing small groups?

Challenge	Ideas
There are so many materials to manage.	• Set up a folder or basket for each group. • Make students responsible for bringing the materials they will need. List those items on the board or a chart. • Keep a set of basic supplies on the small group table.
I don't dare turn my back on the rest of the class. I need to take time from the small group to deal with discipline issues in the larger group.	• Put the back of your chair to the wall to keep you facing the rest of the class. • Position a chart or board near you and write a number from one to five, with five representing exemplary behavior. Quietly adjust the number for all to see. Compliment the class for the number of fours and fives they have at the end of the work time.
Some students get distracted by the movements or conversations of others.	• Set up a "Silent Zone" for students who need to work with few distractions. A divider can help define spaces. • Help students see that having the ability to focus is a skill that they can practice and improve over time.
I don't want to waste time between groups.	• List the names of students in each of the groups that day in a place for all to see. • Give a "two-minute warning" as you wrap up work with one group. Tell the next group that they have two minutes to gather their materials to get ready for their group.

How can I manage the planning for small groups more effectively?

Careful planning can help small group time go more smoothly, yet being flexible when adjustments are needed is a hallmark of a good teacher. Because groupings change based on students' needs, keeping track of specific needs can be a challenge.

In the previous chapter, we looked at some of the assessment options that are useful when determining what skills and strategies students need. As instruction continues, you will constantly need to assess and adjust based on students' reactions and progress.

Effective planning includes:

- Forming groups based on identified strengths and needs
- Matching texts to readers based on ability and interest
- Preparing for explicit teaching of strategies that move students toward independence
- Having materials ready and organized
- Following a predictable structure and flow that allows students to feel comfortable and know what to expect
- Providing opportunities for students to spend large quantities of time reading and writing
- Using checklists, charts, or diagrams that help you track plans and progress
- Setting up systems to manage materials and supplies
- Ensuring that students who are not part of the small group are engaged in purposeful tasks
- Preparing to teach several strategies, as needed, for each skill
- Predetermining how students will demonstrate progress and mastery

Small Group Teaching Points

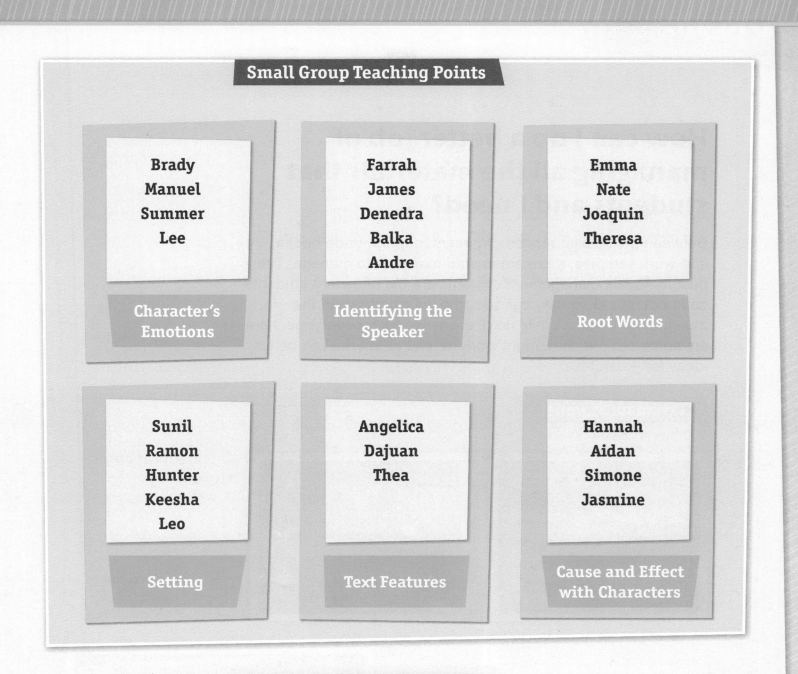

Brady
Manuel
Summer
Lee

Character's Emotions

Farrah
James
Denedra
Balka
Andre

Identifying the Speaker

Emma
Nate
Joaquin
Theresa

Root Words

Sunil
Ramon
Hunter
Keesha
Leo

Setting

Angelica
Dajuan
Thea

Text Features

Hannah
Aidan
Simone
Jasmine

Cause and Effect with Characters

Skill and Strategy Planner

Skill	Strategies
Character's Emotions	• Make the character's facial expressions • Look for feeling words • See how feelings change
Identifying the Speaker	• Find the storyteller • Look for the ''I'' • Hear the voice from an outsider

How can I do a better job of managing all the materials that students and I need?

Between the leveled readers, markers, papers, trade books, and work samples, there are myriad materials to manage. The best materials management systems are the ones that students can understand so they can become your partners in the management tasks. While no one way works for everyone, here are some options that might work for you or spark even better ideas for your class.

Classroom Supplies

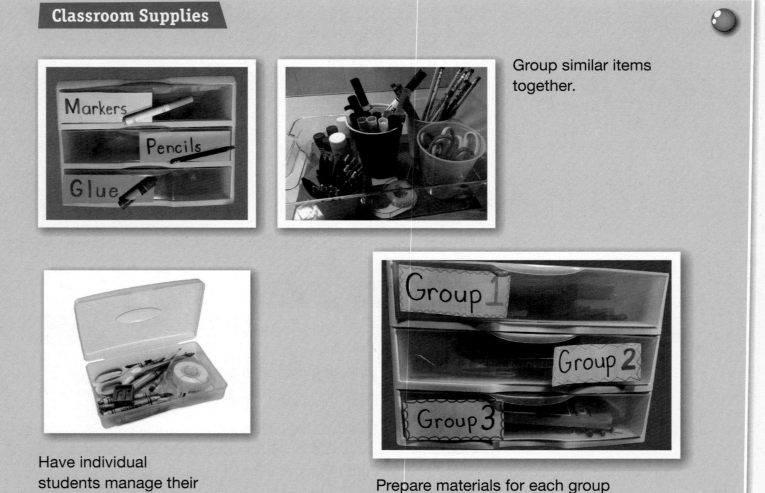

Group similar items together.

Have individual students manage their own supplies.

Prepare materials for each group in advance.

Books

Manage leveled texts or theme books with colorful bins or boxes.

Student Work

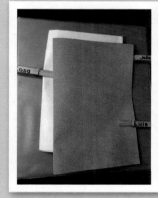

Establish a place for students to turn in work and a system to quickly tell who has not completed a task.

Use binders, folders, boxes, or large envelopes for students to save exemplary work.

What are some ways to maximize my time with students?

While there never seems to be enough time to get everything done that you hope to do, saving a few minutes here and there can add up. Planning for smoother transitions, fewer interruptions, and not needing to repeat instructions can maximize the time you have.

Transitions

Your Choice □ Reading	Writing ✏ Station	Word A₆ᶜ Work	Group Work with Ms. Pradham
Group 1	Group 2	Group 3	Group 4
Group 2	Group 3	Group 4	Group 1
Group 3	Group 4	Group 1	Group 2
Group 4	Group 1	Group 2	Group 3

Give students a visual reminder of what groups they are in and what the groups will be doing throughout the period.

Quiet music can help make transitions calmer.

Create a sign to let students know when they will be in the next small group. This gives them time to gather materials and come to the group prepared.

Interruptions

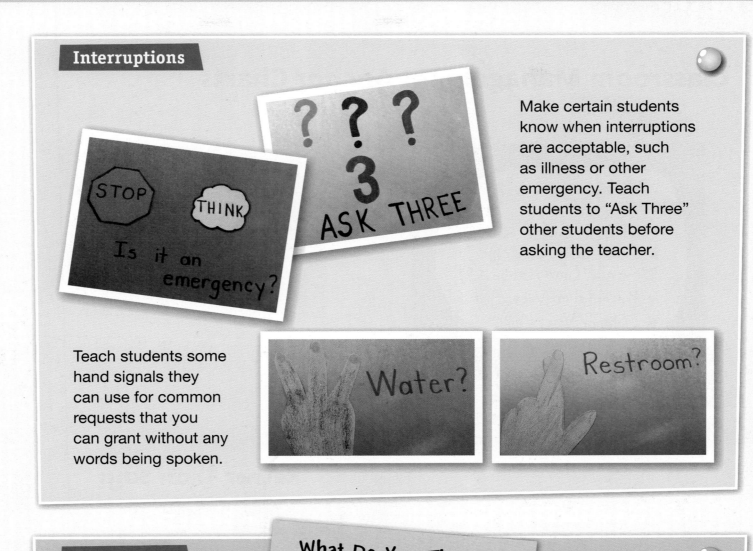

Make certain students know when interruptions are acceptable, such as illness or other emergency. Teach students to "Ask Three" other students before asking the teacher.

Teach students some hand signals they can use for common requests that you can grant without any words being spoken.

Instructions

Create instructions charts with students before having them work independently. Give each activity a name and post the chart where it can be easily referenced. Highlight key action words.

What Do You Think?

1. Think of a survey question.
2. Survey ten people.
3. Graph your results.
4. Write a summary.

Encourage students to repeat the instructions to a partner to check for understanding.

First, we need to think of a survey question. We can write it down.

Classroom Management Anchor Charts

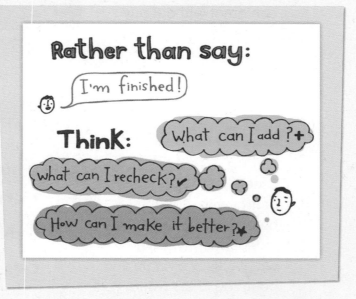

Working Together

How does *myView* support me in planning for, and managing, my small groups?

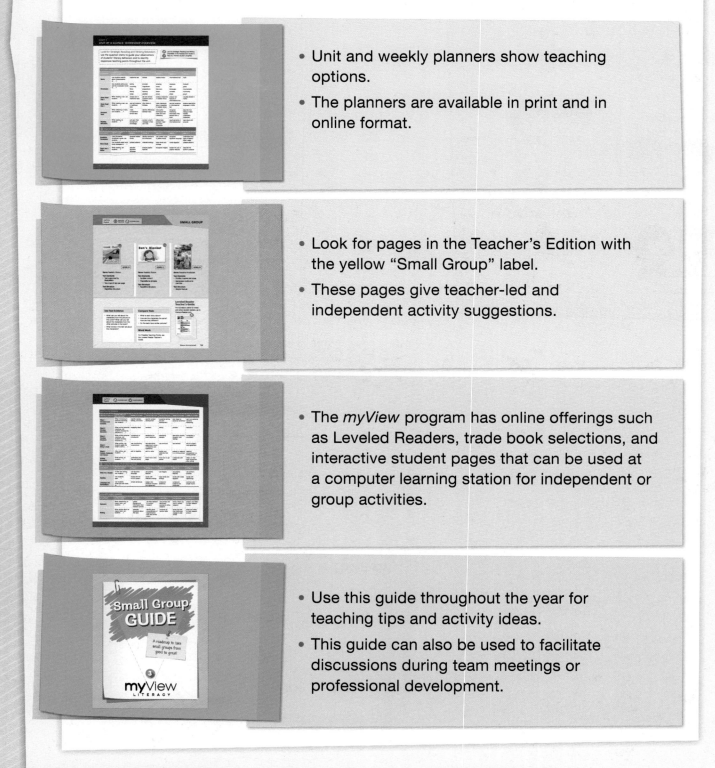

- Unit and weekly planners show teaching options.
- The planners are available in print and in online format.

- Look for pages in the Teacher's Edition with the yellow "Small Group" label.
- These pages give teacher-led and independent activity suggestions.

- The *myView* program has online offerings such as Leveled Readers, trade book selections, and interactive student pages that can be used at a computer learning station for independent or group activities.

- Use this guide throughout the year for teaching tips and activity ideas.
- This guide can also be used to facilitate discussions during team meetings or professional development.

Chapter 4

Small Groups in Action

Questions Addressed in This Chapter

- How can I ensure quality learning in small groups?
- What is a standard framework for small group instruction?
- What is my role in small group instruction?
- How can I facilitate groups and connect with each student?
- What records should I keep about progress in small groups?
- What resources in *myView* help me facilitate small groups?

How can I make certain the whole class stays engaged in meaningful work?

by Judy Wallis, Ed.D. Lecturer, University of Houston and Jim Cummins (ELL), Ph.D. Professor Emeritus, University of Toronto

What differentiates high-quality small group instruction from average instruction?

By organizing groups of 4–6 students who are similar as readers, we have an opportunity to note the common needs of students in a small group. In a similar way, teachers are also able to observe readers' growing proficiency in applying reading skills and strategies. While this close-up view is important for all readers, it is particularly important for striving readers. Too often in large-group teaching, we miss the subtle but important-to-note moves our students make. The close proximity of students and the smaller number of students offers both an opportunity for formative assessment and a chance to turn that assessment immediately into responsive teaching through side-by-side instruction and coaching.

What are some ways to use small groups to provide higher quality instruction for my students who are at various levels of acquiring English?

When mixed English ability or common interest groups are formed, teachers can communicate high expectations to all the groups and provide support to the groups to undertake imaginative projects that express and reinforce students' academic identities. The goal should be to promote identities of confidence and competence among students.

Small group work provides opportunities for teachers to interact with students at a personal level and to develop a deeper understanding of students' personalities, interests, and academic abilities.

What is a common challenge teachers face in providing high-quality instruction in small groups?

Some students simply need more support—more time with a teacher—while other students need more time to engage in supported independent reading, particularly as readers are developing into more proficient readers. The beauty of small group teaching is its flexibility; we can adjust groups as readers grow and change in their needs.

Research tells us that reading volume begins to play an increasingly important role in growing proficient as a reader. For that reason, time to read independently needs to be carved out every day. Students may continue to need help in selecting books, but we know that choice plays a key role in engagement.

What is the role of leveled text in small group instruction?

Leveling systems have been devised to support the text choices we make for students. The use of leveled texts helps us, as teachers, match students with books that are right for them.

As teachers, we keep in mind that leveling systems are designed not as labels for children but rather as scaffolds for us as educators. For all readers, it is important to consider balancing the decoding and comprehension demands within any text. When decoding takes too much cognitive energy, students are unable to think about big ideas and meaning. What we know about reading is that the more students engage in reading accessible text, the better readers they become. As the texts grow more challenging, teachers find small group instruction allows them time to focus on the demands of reading a particular genre, the application of comprehension strategies, and vocabulary and word work.

While I may want to use modifications to make small group instruction work for my class, what is the general framework for it in a workshop classroom?

Ms. Wilkerson has been using small groups successfully in her classroom. She was asked some questions that many teachers have.

Question: How do you get your language arts time started?

Answer: I usually begin with a short whole class introduction. I might teach a minilesson or involve the class in some shared reading or writing. During this whole class time, I remind students what they will be doing while I'm working with groups.

Question: Do all your small groups work in the same way?

Answer: I have different types of groups. Some groups might work on strategies that connect to what I introduced to the whole class while some groups target students who need intervention or enrichment. Some groups focus on conversing about what we have read and prepare for writing.

When I do a guided reading group, the text is usually at their instructional level. When I'm focusing on practicing a new strategy, I try to use text at their independent level. If I'm introducing a skill to a group they might work a little longer than when I'm checking in with them to guide their practice of the skill.

Question: What skills are you teaching more of or less of than in years past?

Answer: Before students can write, they need to have thought about what they have heard or read and what they want to say or write. I'm trying to explicitly teach speaking and listening skills more this year. I think it has helped students' writing a lot. I'm also working on teaching students how to build their reading and writing stamina.

A Common Sequence for Small Group Work

Launch

- I like to begin by complimenting the group on the last skill or concept they learned. I try then to connect that past skill to the new skill.
- I clearly state the purpose of what the group will be doing. It is much like stating the agenda for a well-run meeting.

Introduce Text

- Sometimes I have all the students in the group using the same text. I do a very quick introduction.
- If I have the students practicing a strategy using different texts, I do a quick check to make sure that they have what they need.

Teach and Check

- I model or demonstrate using the skill. I help students understand how it will help them be better readers and writers.
- I have students look through their text and then we find opportunities to see where that skill can be helpful. I check for understanding.

Strategies

- Teaching strategies to master the skill is like giving a new cook a recipe. The strategies have specific steps to follow until they are confident in using the skill without even thinking about the steps.
- I work with the group to create an anchor chart. This visual reminder serves as a support as students practice.

Word Study

- Focusing on individual words helps them keep foundational skills sharp. I point out roots that we can use to form new words, focus on an author's word choices, and make connections to other skills.
- I want my students to not only see the big picture and grasp the gist of the text, but to also look closely and learn from individual words. This is especially helpful in improving their writing.

Connections

- I end my small groups by making several connections. I connect what they have learned to becoming better readers and writers. I also connect to what their follow-up tasks are and how those tasks connect to what they have learned.
- Sending the students off with a compliment about something they did well during the small group time ends the lesson on a positive note.

What is a strategy group, and what happens during that small group time?

PURPOSE:

A strategy group is formed to provide support for students working on a specific skill. Strategies are actions or steps used to help readers and writers accomplish a skill or task. Instructions for these strategies are explicit and focused.

PROCEDURES:

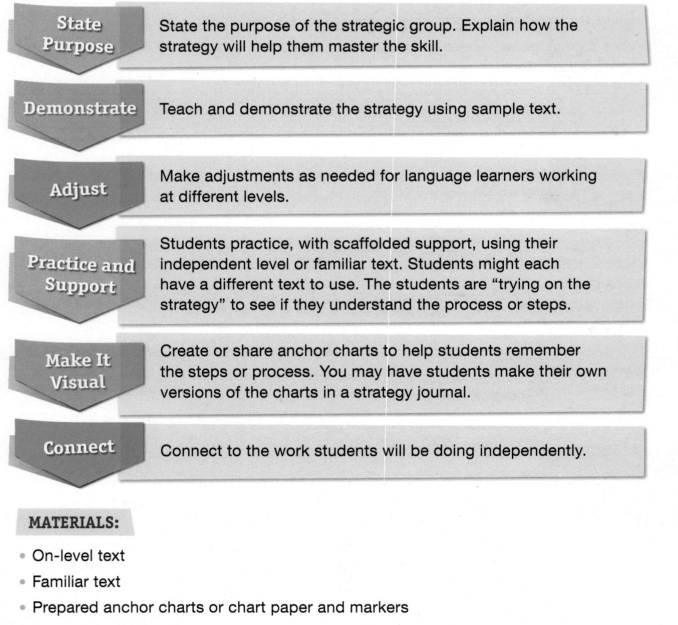

State Purpose	State the purpose of the strategic group. Explain how the strategy will help them master the skill.
Demonstrate	Teach and demonstrate the strategy using sample text.
Adjust	Make adjustments as needed for language learners working at different levels.
Practice and Support	Students practice, with scaffolded support, using their independent level or familiar text. Students might each have a different text to use. The students are "trying on the strategy" to see if they understand the process or steps.
Make It Visual	Create or share anchor charts to help students remember the steps or process. You may have students make their own versions of the charts in a strategy journal.
Connect	Connect to the work students will be doing independently.

MATERIALS:

- On-level text
- Familiar text
- Prepared anchor charts or chart paper and markers
- Strategy journals

What happens in a typical on-level small group?

PURPOSE:

You may use small groups to work with students who are performing on-level to teach strategies or to guide practice on skills introduced during minilessons, shared reading, or shared writing.

PROCEDURES:

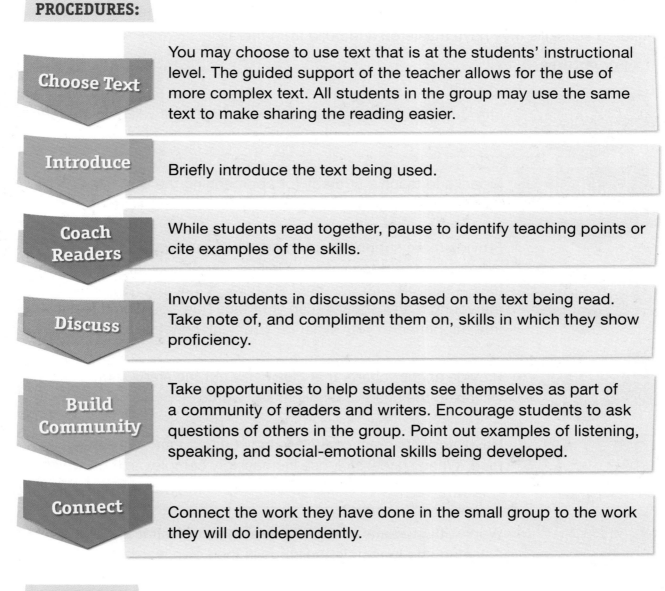

Choose Text
You may choose to use text that is at the students' instructional level. The guided support of the teacher allows for the use of more complex text. All students in the group may use the same text to make sharing the reading easier.

Introduce
Briefly introduce the text being used.

Coach Readers
While students read together, pause to identify teaching points or cite examples of the skills.

Discuss
Involve students in discussions based on the text being read. Take note of, and compliment them on, skills in which they show proficiency.

Build Community
Take opportunities to help students see themselves as part of a community of readers and writers. Encourage students to ask questions of others in the group. Point out examples of listening, speaking, and social-emotional skills being developed.

Connect
Connect the work they have done in the small group to the work they will do independently.

MATERIALS:

- Text at students' instructional level
- Same text for all members of the group

How should I modify groups for intervention?

PURPOSE:

From time to time, any student in the class may need intervention. While working on the same skills as other students, you may need to adjust the amount of support and scaffolding based on needs.

The goal is to have all students master the grade-level expectations. When working with students who are struggling with a skill, identify the related subskills they have mastered and build from there.

PROCEDURES:

Introduce
Introduce the skill and explain how mastering it will help students become better readers and writers.

Model and Teach
Model and teach a strategy for approaching the skill. Perhaps model with several different texts or examples.

Support
Provide more supportive prompts when guiding practice. For example, rather than saying, "Tell me about how the young man feels," support with a prompt such as, "What just happened to the young man? Show me on your face how you would feel if that happened to you. What do you think he feels?"

Make It Visual
Provide anchor charts that clearly lay out the steps. Add visuals to the chart or highlight key words.

Practice
Have students practice the strategy on text that they can easily read. When successful, use increasingly complex text on which they practice the strategy.

Personalize
Work with students to add the strategies to a strategy journal. Ask students to restate the steps in their own words.

MATERIALS:

- Text that the student can read easily
- Anchor charts
- Strategy journals

What modification should I make for students who need enrichment or more advanced work?

PURPOSE:

Every learner can learn a skill at a deeper, more complex level. For example, the skill of identifying a character's emotions can be made more complex when reading text that forces the reader to infer the emotions, rather than reading direct statements in the text. Rather than focusing on more advanced skills, help students become masters of the skills using a variety of more complex texts.

PROCEDURES:

The goal is to have students apply the grade-level skills in increasingly complex texts.

Introduce	Introduce and model the skill. Ask students to suggest how the skill is useful when reading and writing.
Guide	Have students use one or more complex texts and ask open-ended questions to guide a discussion of how the skill can be applied to the texts.
Discuss	Ask students to explain their thinking and provide evidence to support their ideas. Encourage making connections across texts.
Make It Visual	Invite students to share strategies they use to apply the skill. Work together to create anchor charts that make those strategies visual for themselves and other students.

MATERIALS:

- Complex texts
- Chart paper and markers
- Strategy journals
- Reflection journals

How can I use small groups to build fluency?

Fluency Defined

Fluency isn't just saying words quickly. It also involves accuracy, intonation or prosody, inflection, phrasing, emphasis, and rate. Fluent readers can more easily comprehend what they are reading. Students need to hear other fluent readers and hear themselves being fluent readers.

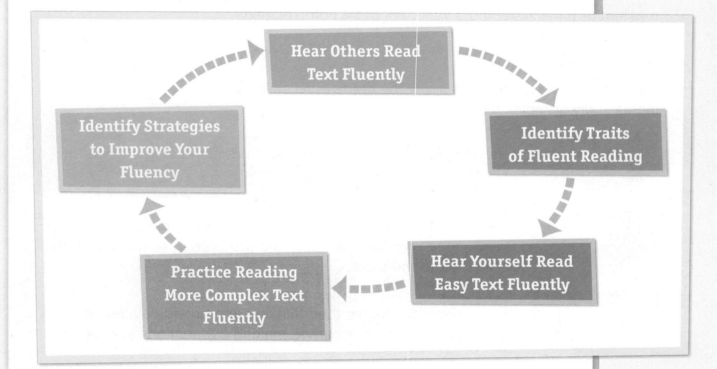

Hear Others Read Text Fluently

Identify Traits of Fluent Reading

Identify Strategies to Improve Your Fluency

Hear Yourself Read Easy Text Fluently

Practice Reading More Complex Text Fluently

Fluency Strategies

- Have students listen to audio recordings of fluent readers. Discuss some of the specific skills that make the reader interesting to listen to as opposed to listening to a robot read the text.

- Invite students to record themselves reading familiar text and self-evaluate the skills they demonstrated and those they need to practice.

- Demonstrate how reading nonfiction as if one is an expert is different than using different voices or expressions when reading a story.

- Practice fluency on short passages more than once. Help students begin to hear themselves become more fluent with each reading of the passage.

What are the roles of leveled texts in small group work?

If a reader is fascinated by a topic, the reader may stretch to comprehend what is being read. If a reader doesn't connect with a text, no matter how simple the words are on the page, the reader won't be encouraged to read more. Matching readers to text is based on both skills and interests.

Fluency Practice
Practice fluency skills on a less-challenging level of text. As skills become more automatic, increase the reading level of the texts.

Strategy Instruction
Use texts at a student's independent reading level to practice new strategies. When those strategies become automatic, move on to more challenging and complex texts.

Uses for Leveled Text

Word Study
Use texts at a student's independent reading level to practice reading accuracy. Use words found in instructional-level texts to expand vocabulary by generating lists of related words.

Independent Practice
Students will use a variety of trade books and leveled texts for independent practice. Students should also have multiple texts available for independent reading and group work.

myView Leveled Readers

Each unit of the *myView* program includes Leveled Readers to assist you in providing leveled texts for students to practice and apply skills and strategies. Reference the "Matching Texts to Learning" pages in the *myView* Teachers Edition for skills and strategies that can be applied to each Leveled Reader. The following pages provide additional information on each Leveled Reader in *myView*. Within any given level of text, the difficulty may also be affected by a student's interest in and familiarity with the genre or subject matter. The text elements and text structure will also serve to make the text more complex or less complex.

Level	The levels are based on Guided Reading Levels. Leveled Readers in the *myView* program range from Level A through Level W.
Lexile®	This score is determined by the sentence length and the frequency of word use. A higher number means the text is more complex.
Genre	Genre may range from familiar narrative fiction stories to more complex informational text. The realism of a fiction or nonfiction narrative or familiarity with the topics can affect the difficulty for the reader. Informational text may contain subject-specific vocabulary that may be unfamiliar to readers.
Text Elements	A close match between the text and the illustrations can make challenging text more understandable. Text elements such as captions and charts can assist students once they are comfortable using them. The use of subtopics or denser formats can challenge readers.
Text Structure	A chronological text structure is often the easiest for readers to follow. Readers will need to learn how to follow other structures as well, such as compare and contrast and descriptive structures.

Information is provided on the following pages for **ALL** the Leveled Readers in the *myView* program, not just for the grade you are currently teaching. You may have students who are reading outside of the range of books expected for the grade. You can access digital versions of any of the Leveled Readers at any grade on PearsonRealize.com.

Grade K UNIT 1				THEME: Going Places	
Title	Level	Lexile®	Genre	Text Elements	Text Structure
At School	A	BR60L	Realistic Fiction	• Familiar content • Predictable sentences	Repetitive Structure
I Ride	A	BR50L	Narrative Nonfiction	• Repeated sentence patterns • One line of text per page	Simple Factual
Our School	A	BR30L	Narrative Nonfiction	• Vocabulary familiar to most students • Short sentences	Simple Factual
A House for a Mouse	A	BR40L	Animal Fantasy	• Text supported by illustrations • Short sentences	Simple Factual
Our Picnic	A	BR60L	Narrative	• Short, predictable sentences • Familiar content	Repetitive Structure
On the Farm	A	BR80L	Narrative Nonfiction	• Text supported by illustrations • Short sentences	Simple Factual
The Zoo	A	BR20L	Realistic Fiction	• Text and concepts supported by illustrations • Short sentences	Repetitive Structure
At the Park	B	70L	Narrative	• Text supported by images • Predictable sentences	Repetitive Structure
At the Beach	B	10L	Narrative	• Familiar vocabulary • Repeating language patterns	Repetitive Structure
Look Out!	B	20L	Realistic Fiction	• Text supported by illustrations • Two lines of text per page	Repetitive Structure
A Mice Hike	B	BR30L	Animal Fantasy	• Vocabulary familiar to most students • Two lines of text per page	Chronological
The Ballpark	B	40L	Narrative	• Text supported by illustrations • Two lines of text per page	Repetitive Structure
My Room	B	120L	Realistic Fiction	• Text and concepts supported by illustrations • Short sentences	Repetitive Structure
Ben's Blanket	C	120L	Realistic Fiction	• Familiar content • Prepositional phrases	Repetitive Structure
The Tea Party	C	170L	Animal Fantasy	• Dialogue • Two to five lines of text per page	Chronological
This is My Home	C	120L	Informational Text	• Vocabulary familiar to most students • Prepositional phrases	Simple Factual
Ant's Hill	D	160L	Animal Fantasy	• Four lines of text per page • Simple dialogue	Repetitive Structure
We Take Care	D	140L	Narrative Nonfiction	• Familiar themes and ideas • Sentences continue to next line	Simple Factual

Grade K UNIT 2				THEME: Living Things	
Title	Level	Lexile®	Genre	Text Elements	Text Structure
My Birthday Party	A	BR10L	Animal Fantasy	• Text highly supported by illustrations	Repetitive Structure
Hello, Birds	A	BR10L	Narrative	• Text supported by illustrations	Repetitive Structure
Baby Bird	A	BR120L	Informational Text	• One line of text per page	Simple Factual
My Pet	A	BR10L	Narrative Nonfiction	• Four words per page	Simple Factual
I Can Help	A	BR80L	Narrative Nonfiction	• Three words per page	Simple Factual
The Garden	A	BR30L	Narrative	• Four words per page	Repetitive Structure
We Eat	A	BR10L	Narrative	• Four words per page	Repetitive Structure
Wake Up!	B	90L	Narrative	• Two lines per page	Repetitive Structure
Cleaning Up	B	110L	Narrative Nonfiction	• Two lines per page	Repetitive Structure
At the Seaside	B	120L	Informational Text	• Two lines per page	Simple Factual
At the Pond	B	0L	Informational Text	• Two lines per page	Simple Factual
How Does It Feel?	B	150L	Informational Text	• Two lines per page	Simple Factual
The Rose Plant	B	140L	Informational Text	• Two lines per page	Simple Factual
Ben's Baby Brother	C	90L	Realistic Fiction	• Two lines per page	Repetitive Structure
Life on the Farm	C	140L	Narrative Nonfiction	• One to three lines per page	Simple Factual
Basic Needs	C	250L	Informational Text	• Two lines per page	Simple Factual
Come Here, Cat	D	160L	Narrative	• Simple dialogue	Chronological
Slow Down, Stooley!	D	180L	Narrative	• Familiar content and ideas	Chronological
Busy Bee	D	160L	Narrative	• Two to four lines of text per page	Chronological

Dig In!

| Grade K | UNIT 3 | THEME: Tell Me a Story |

Title	Level	Lexile®	Genre	Text Elements	Text Structure
Draw a Dog	A	BR50L	Narrative Nonfiction	• Repeating language patterns	Simple Factual
I Like Stories	A	BR70L	Narrative	• Three to five words per page	Repetitive Structure
Roll the Dough	A	BR40L	Narrative	• Repeated sentence patterns • One line of text per page	Repetitive Structure
Story Time!	A	BR60L	Narrative	• Text supported by illustrations • Short sentences	Repetitive Structure
Paper Chains	A	BR40L	Nonfiction	• One line of text per page	Simple Factual
I Can Move!	A	BR110L	Narrative Nonfiction	• One line of text per page	Simple Factual
Time for a Story	B	50L	Animal Fantasy	• Text supported by illustrations • Two lines of text per page	Repetitive Structure
Look At Me!	B	60L	Narrative	• Two lines of text per page	Repetitive Structure
This Is a Dancer	B	40L	Nonfiction	• Predictable sentences	Simple Factual
They All Play	B	110L	Animal Fantasy	• Two lines of text per page	Repetitive Structure
A Play	B	120L	Informational Text	• Predictable sentences	Repetitive Structure
Tracks in the Snow	B	150L	Informational Text	• Text highly supported by illustrations	Simple Factual
The Library Book	C	200L	Narrative	• Three lines per page	Repetitive Structure
Yaya's First Play	C	110L	Narrative	• Most vocabulary familiar to readers	Repetitive Structure
Our Elders	C	120L	Narrative Nonfiction	• Two lines of text per page	Repetitive Structure
A Story for Leo	D	180L	Narrative	• Some sentences turn to next line	Chronological
Full of Stories	D	200L	Narrative	• Easy content and ideas	Chronological
Drawing Stories	D	170L	Informational Text	• Familiar, easy content	Simple Factual

| Grade K | UNIT 4 | THEME: Then and Now |

Title	Level	Lexile®	Genre	Text Elements	Text Structure
Mouse Pictures	B	10L	Animal Fantasy	• Predictable sentences	Repetitive Structure
In the Museum	B	50L	Narrative Nonfiction	• Predictable sentences	Simple Factual
Build a Tower	B	80L	Narrative	• One to two lines of text per page	Repetitive Structure
Merry Christmas	B	90L	Narrative Nonfiction	• Predictable sentences	Simple Factual
Chinese New Year	B	120L	Narrative Nonfiction	• Predictable sentences	Simple Factual
Family Teachers	B	20L	Informational Text	• Text highly supported by illustrations	Simple Factual
I Can	C	60L	Narrative	• Two lines of text per page	Repetitive Structure
Chimp School	C	170L	Informational Text	• Exclamation points	Simple Factual
Fire! Fire!	C	120L	Informational Text	• Prepositional phrases	Simple Factual
Ready for School	C	60L	Informational Text	• Familiar content	Simple Factual
A Long Time Ago	C	190L	Informational Text	• Prepositional phrases	Simple Factual
The Suitcase	D	180L	Animal Fantasy	• Easy content and ideas	Repetitive Structure
Nana and Ruby	D	170L	Narrative	• Simple dialogue	Chronological
I Am Here	D	140L	Narrative	• Familiar, easy content	Repetitive Structure
Time to Eat	D	170L	Narrative	• Simple dialogue	Repetitive Structure
Rosh Hashanah	D	170L	Narrative Nonfiction	• Familiar, easy content	Simple Factual

Grade K — UNIT 5 — THEME: Outside My Door

Title	Level	Lexile®	Genre	Text Elements	Text Structure
Leaves	B	50L	Narrative	• Two lines of text per page	Repetitive Structure
Where Is the Rain?	B	50L	Narrative Nonfiction	• Predictable sentences	Simple Factual
Let's Go!	B	40L	Narrative	• Two lines of text per page	Repetitive Structure
Seasons	B	150L	Informational Text	• Two lines of text per page	Simple Factual
At Night	B	140L	Informational Text	• Predictable sentences	Simple Factual
What Will I Wear Today?	B	170L	Narrative Nonfiction	• Two lines of text per page	Simple Factual
The Wind	C	150L	Narrative	• Three lines of text per page	Repetitive Structure
California	C	260L	Informational Text	• Predictable sentences	Simple Factual
I See a Sheep	C	170L	Narrative	• Three lines of text per page	Repetitive Structure
Henry Looks Up	C	170L	Narrative	• Three lines of text per page	Repetitive Structure
A Very Hot Day	C	170L	Narrative	• Predictable sentences	Repetitive Structure
What Do the Clouds Say Today?	C	170L	Informational Text	• Two lines of text per page	Repetitive Structure
The Storm	D	190L	Narrative	• Familiar, easy content	Repetitive Structure
Rocks Around Us	D	220L	Informational Text	• Familiar, easy content	Simple Factual
Animals in the Rain	D	210L	Informational Text	• Some sentences go to next line	Simple Factual
Thunderbird	D	180L	Traditional	• Some sentences go to next line	Repetitive Structure
Rainbows	D	370L	Informational Text	• Familiar, easy content	Simple Factual
Three Little Kittens	D	400L	Traditional	• Simple and split dialogue	Chronological
Go Outside!	D	200L	Informational Text	• Some sentences go to next line	Simple Factual

Grade 1 — UNIT 1 — THEME: My Neighborhood

Title	Level	Lexile®	Genre	Text Elements	Text Structure
A Garden	B	130L	Informational Text	• Text highly supported by pictures	Simple Factual
Hide-and-Seek	B	40L	Animal Fantasy	• Text highly supported by pictures	Repetitive Structure
Shapes in My World	B	20L	Narrative Nonfiction	• Text highly supported by pictures	Repetitive Structure
The Blue House	C	120L	Fantasy	• Familiar, easy content	Repetitive Structure
Let's Make Lemonade	C	150L	Realistic Fiction	• Prepositional phrases	Chronological
Homes	C	140L	Narrative Nonfiction	• Prepositional phrases	Repetitive Structure
Sarah's Surprise	D	230L	Realistic Fiction	• Easy content and ideas	Repetitive Structure
Run, Rusty! Run!	D	210L	Realistic Fiction	• Simple dialogue	Chronological
Earth Day	D	250L	Informational Text	• Complex spelling patterns	Description
Parades	E	390L	Informational Text	• Easy content and ideas	Description
Community Cook-Off	E	330L	Realistic Fiction	• Easy content and ideas	Chronological
Fourth of July	E	270L	Realistic Fiction	• Concepts supported by illustrations	Chronological
Our Community Center	F	370L	Narrative Nonfiction	• Prepositional phrases	Description
Zoom to the Moon	F	280L	Fantasy	• Simple and split dialogue	Chronological
Follow the Rules	F	480L	Realistic Fiction	• Simple and split dialogue	Chronological
Treasure Hunting	G	450L	Informational Text	• Some sequential information	Description
Too Hot!	G	470L	Realistic Fiction	• Sentences with clauses	Chronological
Good Neighbors	G	450L	Informational Text	• Familiar content	Description
Yard Sale	H	460L	Realistic Fiction	• Some complex letter-sound relationships	Chronological
We Celebrate Together	H	500L	Narrative Nonfiction	• Complex spelling patterns	Compare and Contrast
Do You Need a Bag?	H	490L	Realistic Fiction	• Easy compound words	Chronological
Hoop Shot	I	490L	Realistic Fiction	• Many two-to-three syllable words	Chronological
Erin's Neighborhood	I	440L	Realistic Fiction	• Many two-to-three syllable words	Chronological
Super Freddie	I	510L	Fantasy	• Many two-to-three syllable words	Chronological

Dig In!

Grade 1 — UNIT 2 — THEME: I Spy

Title	Level	Lexile®	Genre	Text Elements	Text Structure
Kittens and Cats	B	130L	Informational Text	• Two lines per page	Simple Factual
Who Am I?	B	130L	Realistic Fiction	• Text supported by illustrations • Two lines of text per page	Repetitive Structure
My Little Sister	B	140L	Realistic Fiction	• Text highly supported by pictures	Repetitive Structure
The Elephant's Trunk	C	40L	Informational Text	• Vocabulary familiar to readers	Repetitive Structure
Where Will We Go?	C	160L	Narrative Nonfiction	• Familiar, easy content	Simple Factual
I Can Change	C	370L	Animal Fantasy	• Two lines per page	Repetitive Structure
A Spider's Web	D	260L	Informational Text	• Familiar, easy content	Description
The Class Pet	D	210L	Informational Text	• Familiar, easy content	Simple Factual
What Will It Be?	D	160L	Realistic Fiction	• Easy content and ideas	Chronological
A Walk in the Woods	E	210L	Narrative Nonfiction	• Easy content and ideas	Description
Let's Grow a Mango	E	240L	Realistic Fiction	• Concepts supported by illustrations	Chronological
Everything Changes	E	260L	Realistic Fiction	• Some longer sentences	Chronological
How Animals Grow	F	360L	Informational Text	• Some sequential information	Description
Our Terrarium	F	330L	Narrative Nonfiction	• Sequential information	Description
Frog Tales	F	480L	Realistic Fiction	• Familiar content	Chronological
A Rainbow of Foods	G	450L	Informational Text	• Familiar content	Description
Ziggy Grows Up	G	330L	Realistic Fiction	• Sentences with clauses	Chronological
Make a Wish	G	440L	Realistic Fiction	• Sentences with clauses	Chronological
Growing Peppers	H	400L	Informational Text	• Accessible content	Sequential
The Dream	H	470L	Realistic Fiction	• Narrative with less repetition	Chronological
Not Yet!	H	470L	Realistic Fiction	• Easy compound words	Chronological
Sharks	I	450L	Informational Text	• Concepts highly supported by text and illustrations	Description
The Mimic Octopus	I	460L	Informational Text	• Two to eight lines per page	Simple Factual
The Bear	I	450L	Realistic Fiction	• More elaborated episodes	Chronological

Grade 1 — UNIT 3 — THEME: Imagine That

Title	Level	Lexile®	Genre	Text Elements	Text Structure
Dress-Up!	B	230L	Realistic Fiction	• Text supported by illustrations • Two lines of text per page	Repetitive Structure
Shadow Puppets	B	30L	Narrative Nonfiction	• One to two lines of text per page	Simple Factual
I Draw With Chalk	B	80L	Realistic Fiction	• Predictable sentences • Two lines of text per page	Repetitive Structure
The Music Men	C	270L	Realistic Fiction	• Three lines of text per page	Repetitive Structure
Let's Build a Fort	C	180L	Realistic Fiction	• Two to three lines of text per page	Repetitive Structure
Let's Make a Mask	C	180L	Informational Text	• Familiar, easy content	Simple Factual
What Is Art?	D	220L	Informational Text	• Familiar, easy content	Simple Factual
The Baseball Hat	D	250L	Fantasy	• Words with inflectional endings	Chronological
Cool Cakes	D	220L	Narrative Nonfiction	• Familiar, easy content	Simple Factual
Chicken Little	E	300L	Folktale	• Variety of words to assign dialogue	Chronological
Costumes	E	230L	Narrative Nonfiction	• Easy content and ideas	Description
Just Dance	E	220L	Procedural-How-to	• Easy content and ideas	Description
Sam's Blue Coat	F	200L	Traditional Stories	• Familiar content	Chronological
Art Around the World	F	460L	Informational Text	• Familiar content expands beyond reader's experience	Description
Donna Mouse in the City	F	370L	Folktale	• Simple and split dialogue	Chronological
The Giant Carrot	G	420L	Folktale	• Sentences with clauses	Chronological
Imagine That!	G	490L	Informational Text	• Familiar content	Compare and Contrast
Cool Buildings	G	400L	Informational Text	• Familiar content	Compare and Contrast
The Duckling	H	420L	Folktale	• Words with complex spelling patterns	Chronological
The Kingdom of Imagination	H	450L	Fantasy	• Multiple episodes	Chronological
What Will I Be?	H	460L	Narrative Nonfiction	• Accessible content	Description
Stone Soup	I	480L	Folktale	• More elaborated episodes	Chronological
The Elves and the Shoemaker	I	470L	Folktale	• More elaborated episodes	Chronological
Media In Our World	I	520L	Informational Text	• Familiar and new content	Compare and Contrast

Grade 1 — UNIT 4 — THEME: Making History

Title	Level	Lexile®	Genre	Text Elements	Text Structure
Welcome Home!	C	160L	Realistic Fiction	• Two to three lines of text per page	Chronological
Pioneer Village	C	330L	Informational Text	• Familiar, easy content	Simple Factual
A Restaurant	C	280L	Informational Text	• Familiar, easy content	Simple Factual
My Grandpa's Stories	D	240L	Realistic Fiction	• Prepositional phrases	Repetitive Structure
Ways to Learn	D	170L	Informational Text	• Familiar, easy content	Simple Factual
In the Past	D	260L	Informational Text	• Familiar, easy content	Simple Factual
When I Live in the White House	E	330L	Fantasy	• Concepts supported by illustrations	Chronological
Moving Day	E	280L	Realistic Fiction	• Simple and split dialogue	Chronological
Cave Paintings	E	280L	Informational Text	• Easy content and ideas	Description
Bones	F	320L	Narrative Nonfiction	• Familiar content expands beyond reader's experience	Description
Treasures Under the Sea	F	290L	Animal Fantasy	• Simple and split dialogue	Chronological
Suzie Goes to School	F	340L	Realistic Fiction	• Simple and split dialogue	Chronological
The Breakfast Party	G	460L	Realistic Fiction	• Concepts supported by illustrations	Chronological
The Boy Who Cried Wolf	G	300L	Folktale	• Concepts supported by illustrations	Chronological
Heroes in the Hills	G	500L	Informational Text	• Heads and other text features	Description
Goods and Services	H	470L	Informational Text	• Accessible content	Description
You Are an Inventor!	H	510L	Realistic Fiction	• Easy compound words	Chronological
Bebe and Bessie in the Clouds	H	460L	Realistic Fiction	• Easy compound words	Chronological
Welcome to America	H	510L	Narrative Nonfiction	• Accessible content	Description
Here's Your Mail	I	500L	Informational Text	• Four to eight lines per page	Simple Factual
Making Maple Syrup	I	450L	Realistic Fiction	• More elaborated episodes	Chronological
Dadi and Grandma	I	500L	Realistic Fiction	• Some concepts supported by illustrations	Chronological
Squirrel's Treasure of Nuts	I	500L	Animal Fantasy	• Some concepts supported by illustrations	Chronological
How Do You Communicate?	I	510L	Informational Text	• Four to eight lines per page	Compare and Contrast

Grade 1 — UNIT 5 — THEME: Beyond My World

Title	Level	Lexile®	Genre	Text Elements	Text Structure
Off To Sleep	D	240L	Animal Fantasy	• Simple dialogue	Chronological
Hello, Spring!	D	200L	Informational Text	• Familiar, easy content	Simple Factual
Hello, Summer!	D	180L	Informational Text	• Prepositional phrases	Simple Factual
Henry and Hops	E	250L	Animal Fantasy	• Simple and split dialogue	Chronological
Hello, Fall!	E	280L	Informational Text	• Easy content and ideas	Simple Factual
Hello, Winter!	E	240L	Informational Text	• Concepts supported by photographs	Simple Factual
All Year Round	F	320L	Realistic Fiction	• Simple and split dialogue	Chronological
Water Adventure	F	270L	Informational Text	• Two to three lines of text per page	Description
Animals on the Move	F	320L	Informational Text	• Two to five lines of text per page	Description
How the Buffalo Came to Be	G	360L	Traditional Story	• Sentences with clauses	Chronological
The Pumpkin Patch	G	440L	Realistic Fiction	• Sentences with clauses	Chronological
Soil	G	400L	Informational Text	• Section heads	Description
The Olympics	G	480L	Informational Text	• Most content carried by the text	Description
Happy Campers	H	510L	Realistic Fiction	• Simple and split dialogue	Chronological
Let's Play!	H	470L	Narrative Nonfiction	• Compound words and prepositional phrases	Description
You Can't Wear That!	H	480L	Animal Fantasy	• Easy compound words	Chronological
The Wonderful Art of Bart	H	470L	Realistic Fiction	• Words with complex spelling patterns	Chronological
The Holiday Seasons	H	500L	Informational Text	• Some concepts supported by photographs	Description
Harvest Time!	I	470L	Informational Text	• Four to eight lines per page	Description
Life at the Lake	I	520L	Realistic Fiction	• Some concepts supported by illustrations	Chronological
Wild Weather	I	500L	Informational Text	• Four to eight lines per page	Description
My Favorite Season	I	480L	Realistic Fiction	• Some concepts supported by illustrations	Chronological
The Ant and the Grasshopper	I	510L	Folktale	• Some concepts supported by illustrations	Chronological
Hibernation	I	480L	Informational Text	• Four to eight lines of text per page	Description

Dig In!

Grade 2	UNIT 1	THEME: You Are Here			
Title	Level	Lexile®	Genre	Text Elements	Text Structure
Captain Cat	H	470L	Animal Fantasy	• Narrative with less repetition • Dialogue assigned to speaker through a variety of words	Chronological
The Knight's Riddle	H	440L	Fairy Tale	• Narrative with less repetition • Three to eight lines per page	Chronological
Continents and Oceans	H	550L	Informational Text	• Content expands beyond home • Some complex spelling patterns	Description
Travel the United States	I	570L	Informational Text	• Table of contents • Mix of familiar and new content	Description
Jerry and Juan	I	470L	Realistic Fiction	• Mix of new and familiar content • Sentences carry over two lines	Chronological
Landmarks of the United States	I	640L	Narrative Nonfiction	• Table of contents • Mix of familiar and new content	Description
Los Angeles Over the Years	J	610L	Informational Text	• Clearly presented organizational structure • Many lines of print per page	Description
Mara Goes Home	J	490L	Animal Fantasy	• Abstract concepts supported by text and illustrations • Many lines of print per page	Chronological
Road Trip	J	490L	Realistic Fiction	• Settings that are unfamiliar to some children • Many lines of print per page	Chronological
Cool Jobs	K	650L	Expository Text	• More complex sentences • Varied organization of information	Compare and Contrast
The Great Sphinx Mystery	K	530L	Mystery	• Varied words to assign dialogue • Words that are challenging to decode	Chronological
Sunlight: A Natural Resource	K	540L	Expository Text	• Varied organization of information • Longer sentences	Description
Adventure on Mount Everest	L	630L	Realistic Fiction	• New vocabulary • Plot and setting outside of typical experience	Chronological
Moving to Florida	L	550L	Realistic Fiction	• New vocabulary • Plot outside of some readers' experience	Chronological
We Live in Communities	L	550L	Informational Text	• Mix of new and familiar content • Sentences carry over two lines	Compare and Contrast
A Fish Out of Water	M	590L	Realistic Fiction	• Meaning conveyed through text rather than images • Multiple points of view shown through characters' behaviors	Chronological
Ivan and the Lost Kitten	M	540L	Realistic Fiction	• Meaning carried by print • Multisyllable words that are challenging to decode	Chronological
Notes From Antarctica	M	610L	Expository Text	• Multisyllable words that are challenging to decode • Content-specific words introduced and explained	Blog Entries

Grade 2	UNIT 2	THEME: Nature's Wonders			
Title	Level	Lexile®	Genre	Text Elements	Text Structure
Daisy and Drake	H	480L	Realistic Fiction	• Three to eight lines per page • Accessible content	Chronological
Nature's Patterns	H	470L	Expository Text	• Easy compound words • Three to eight lines per page	Compare and Contrast
We Make Patterns	H	510L	Expository Text	• Some easy compound words • Three to eight lines per page	Compare and Contrast
Time to Hibernate	I	470L	Animal Fantasy	• Mix of familiar and new content • Sentences carry over two to three lines	Chronological
The Monarch Butterfly	I	500L	Expository Text	• Table of contents • Longer sentences carry over two lines	Description
Batter Up!	I	480L	Realistic Fiction	• Mix of familiar and new content • Sentences carry over two to three lines	Chronological
Night Magic	J	530L	Realistic Fiction	• Some ideas new to readers • Some settings new to many readers	Chronological
Polar Animals	J	530L	Expository Text	• Settings that are unfamiliar to some children • Many lines of print per page	Description
Plants of the Sonoran Desert	J	530L	Expository Text	• Some ideas new to readers • Many lines of print per page	Description
Lobo Returns	K	480L	Realistic Fiction	• Situations unfamiliar to many readers • Variety of words used to assign dialogue	Chronological
The Underground Crowd	K	560L	Informational Text	• Longer, more complex sentences • Varied organization	Compare and Contrast
Campfire Stories	K	520L	Mystery	• Longer, more complex sentences • Variety of words used to assign dialogue	Story within Story
Earth's Waters	L	620L	Expository Text	• Table of contents, glossary, and index • Longer sentences carry over three lines	Description
Happy Diwali!	L	550L	Realistic Fiction	• Mix of new and familiar content • Sentences carry over multiple lines	Chronological
Big Changes	L	550L	Expository Text	• Table of contents, glossary, and index • Longer sentences carry over three lines	Compare and Contrast
Eerie Cavern	M	530L	Animal Fantasy	• Most content carried by text • Characters revealed through behavior	Chronological
Amazing Migrations	M	560L	Expository Text	• Most content carried by text • Some new vocabulary explained in text	Compare and Contrast
Water's Journey	M	550L	Expository Text	• Most content carried by text • Multisyllable words that are challenging to decode	Sequential

Grade 2	UNIT 3	THEME: Our Traditions			
Title	Level	Lexile®	Genre	Text Elements	Text Structure
The Horn	H	450L	Fantasy	• Three to eight lines per page • Minimal illustration	Chronological
The Beat	H	450L	Narrative	• Three to eight lines per page • Accessible content	Chronological
Dancing Around	H	540L	Informational Text	• Some easy compound words • Accessible content from beyond readers' home	Compare and Contrast
The Greedy Dog	I	480L	Folktale	• Three-syllable words • Sentences carry over two to three lines	Chronological
When I Was Eight	I	510L	Narrative	• Longer stretches of dialogue • Five to eight lines of text per page	Chronological
Pass It On	I	540L	Expository Text	• Table of contents • Mix of familiar and new content	Description
Moon Cakes	J	520L	Folktale	• Settings that are unfamiliar to some children • Many lines of print per page	Chronological
Game On!	J	570L	Informational Text	• Clearly presented organizational structure • Many lines of print per page	Description
Traditions Around the World	J	540L	Informational Text	• Some ideas new to most readers • Many lines of print per page	Compare and Contrast
Weighing an Elephant	K	580L	Folktale	• Situations unfamiliar to many readers • Variety of words used to assign dialogue	Chronological
Celebrate with Food	K	620L	Informational Text	• Longer, more complex sentences • Varied organization	Compare and Contrast
Three Wishes	K	540L	Traditional	• Longer, more complex sentences • Variety of words used to assign dialogue	Chronological
The Magic Millstone	L	510L	Legend	• Plot and situation outside typical experience • Sentences carry over multiple lines	Chronological
Happy New Year!	L	560L	Informational Text	• Table of contents, glossary, and index • Longer sentences carry over three lines	Compare and Contrast
Traditional Clothing	L	570L	Informational Text	• Multisyllable words • Some new vocabulary explained in text	Description
The Big Swim	M	560L	Realistic Fiction	• Meaning conveyed through text rather than images • Multisyllable words that are challenging to decode	Chronological
The Crafty Fox	M	630L	Folktale	• Most content carried by text • Characters revealed through behavior	Chronological
Learning About Traditions	M	640L	Nonfiction	• Most content carried by text • Multisyllable words that are challenging to decode	Description with Travel Diaries

Grade 2	UNIT 4	THEME: Making a Difference			
Title	Level	Lexile®	Genre	Text Elements	Text Structure
How Loose Is Your Tooth?	I	500L	Realistic Fiction	• Two-to-three syllable words • Sentences carry over two to three lines	Chronological
Celebrating Eid	I	490L	Realistic Fiction	• Familiar and new content • Five to eight lines of text per page	Chronological
Helping Your Community	I	530L	Expository Text	• Table of contents • Multisyllable words	Compare and Contrast
Show-and-Tell	J	500L	Narrative	• Complex letter-sound relationships • Many lines of print per page	Chronological
Who's Calling?	J	550L	Narrative Nonfiction	• Some ideas new to most readers • Many lines of print per page	Description
Flags	J	520L	Informational Text	• Some ideas new to most readers • Many lines of print per page	Description
Freddy Forget-Me-Not Loses His Laugh	K	540L	Fantasy	• Longer, more complex sentences • Variety of words used to assign dialogue	Chronological
Dear Diary	K	550L	Realistic Fiction	• Longer, more complex sentences • Variety of words used to assign dialogue	Chronological with Diary Entries
Together We Give Thanks	K	600L	Narrative Nonfiction	• Longer, more complex sentences • Varied organization	Description
Let's Talk	K	560L	Expository Text	• Longer, more complex sentences • Varied organization	Description
Sam's Stones	L	540L	Realistic Fiction	• Challenging multisyllable words • New, unexplained vocabulary	Chronological with Flashback
Milo's Basketball	L	520L	Realistic Fiction	• Challenging multisyllable words • Sentences carry over multiple lines	Chronological
Mary Ann Shadd: Fighting for Change	L	650L	Narrative Nonfiction	• Some new vocabulary explained in the text • Challenging multisyllable words	Description
Franklin Delano Roosevelt: A People's Leader	L	640L	Narrative Nonfiction	• Table of contents, glossary, and index • Longer sentences carry over three lines	Description
Cool Clubs	M	620L	Informational Text	• Most content carried by text • Multisyllable words that are challenging to decode	Compare and Contrast
Independence Day	M	650L	Narrative Nonfiction	• Most content carried by text • Multisyllable words that are challenging to decode	Description
Strength in Numbers	M	630L	Narrative Nonfiction	• Some new vocabulary explained in the text • Most content carried by text	Compare and Contrast
Grandpa Don's New Home	M	550L	Realistic Fiction	• Content carried by print • Multiple characters to understand	Chronological

Dig In!

Grade 2 — UNIT 5 — THEME: Our Incredible Earth

Title	Level	Lexile®	Genre	Text Elements	Text Structure
Amazing Animal Builders	J	490L	Procedural-How-to	• Some ideas new to most readers • Many lines of print per page	Compare and Contrast
Glaciers	J	540L	Informational Text	• Some concepts supported by images • Chapter titles, glossary, and index	Description
Freeze-Frame	J	530L	Realistic Fiction	• Abstract concepts supported by illustrations • Many lines of print per page	Chronological
Kya and the Sea	K	520L	Adventure	• Longer, more complex sentences • Content carried by print	Chronological
The Parakeet Gem	K	540L	Mystery	• Longer, more complex sentences • Chapter titles	Chronological
Logging Our Forests	K	570L	Informational Text	• Varied organization of information • Sentences of more than fifteen words	Description
Technology: Then and Now	K	640L	Informational Text	• Varied organization of information • Sentences of more than fifteen words	Compare and Contrast
Guroop and the Ocean Tides	L	540L	Realistic Fiction	• Content carried by print • Sentences carry over multiple lines	Chronological
At the Weather Station	L	540L	Realistic Fiction	• Challenging multisyllable words • Sentences carry over multiple lines	Chronological
The Pirate Map	L	550L	Realistic Fiction	• Challenging multisyllable words • Content carried by print	Chronological
Our Changing Earth	L	600L	Informational Text	• Table of contents, glossary, and index • Variety of text features	Description
The Rising Seas	L	560L	Informational Text	• Some new vocabulary explained in text • Challenging multisyllable words	Description
The Buried Beach	M	540L	Realistic Fiction	• Content carried by print • Multiple characters to understand	Chronological
Artificial Islands	M	640L	Informational Text	• Some new vocabulary explained in the text • Variety of text features	Description
Continents on the Move	M	570L	Informational Text	• Some new vocabulary explained in the text • Diagrams and maps	Description
Objects in Space	M	640L	Informational Text	• New vocabulary defined in the text or glossary • Variety of text features	Description
Magnificent Magnets	M	550L	Informational Text	• New vocabulary defined in the text or glossary • Diagrams	Description
Lisa and Lucas in the Forest	M	570L	Realistic Fiction	• Some new vocabulary defined in context • Multiple characters to understand	Chronological

Grade 3 — UNIT 1 — THEME: Environments

Title	Level	Lexile®	Genre	Text Elements	Text Structure
All-Weather Friends	L	540L	Realistic Fiction	• Some new vocabulary • Multisyllable words	Chronological with Letters
The Letter	L	530L	Mystery	• Situations outside typical experience • Dialogue assigned in a variety of ways	Chronological
Living in Different Environments	L	740L	Informational Text	• Decoding challenges • Some new terms explained in text	Compare and Contrast
Inuit Life	M	720L	Procedural	• Most content conveyed by print • Some new vocabulary introduced and explained in text	Description
Pine Is Special	M	670L	Traditional Story	• Abstract themes • Most content carried by text	Chronological
Welcome to Tonle Sap!	M	770L	Informational Text	• Most content carried by text • Multisyllable words	Description
The Greatest Adventure	N	640L	Historical Fiction	• Complex plots with time passing • Multiple characters to follow	Chronological with Journal Entries
It's Snowing	N	540L	Realistic Fiction	• Characters' attributes shown in various ways • Varying sentence length and complexity	Chronological
Pollution	N	770L	Informational Text	• Presentation of multiple subtopics • Prefixes and suffixes	Description
High-Speed Adventure	O	770L	Science Fiction	• Multiple characters to follow • Figurative language	Chronological
In Short Supply	O	820L	Informational Text	• Multiple subtopics • Some content builds on prior knowledge	Description
Seeds of Peace and Hope	O	810L	Biography	• Multiple subtopics • Some content builds on prior knowledge	Description
Too Scared to Move	P	750L	Realistic Fiction	• Characters revealed by what they say and do • Extensive use of descriptive language	Chronological
Blue Zones	P	810L	Informational Text	• Themes of cultural diversity • Content-specific words defined in text	Compare and Contrast
The Land and the Town	P	790L	Myth/Traditional Story	• Themes of cultural diversity • Descriptive text necessary to understanding the plot	Chronological

Grade 3	UNIT 2	THEME: Interactions			
Title	Level	Lexile®	Genre	Text Elements	Text Structure
Tree Dwellers	L	630L	Informational Text	• Some new vocabulary explained in the text • Challenging multisyllable words	Description
A Home for a Chicken	L	570L	Realistic Fiction	• Some new vocabulary • Multisyllable words	Chronological
Arctic Plants and Animals	L	730L	Informational Text	• Some new vocabulary explained in the text • Challenging multisyllable words	Description
Hummingbird's Garden	M	630L	Animal Fantasy	• Most content carried by text • Multisyllable words	Chronological
Animals of the Everglades	M	730L	Informational Text	• Most content carried by text • Multisyllable words	Description
Swamp City Rumble	M	590L	Animal Fantasy	• Most content carried by text • Multisyllable words	Chronological
A Buzzing Problem	N	720L	Animal Fantasy	• Multiple characters to understand • Sentences of varying length and complexity	Chronological
Staying Alive	N	810L	Informational Text	• Many three-syllable words • Some new vocabulary explained in the text	Description
Bees Around the World	N	750L	Informational Text	• Many three-syllable words • Some new vocabulary explained in the text	Description
One Day in the Garden	O	600L	Animal Fantasy	• Multiple characters to follow • Figurative language	Chronological
African Adventure	O	720L	Realistic Fiction	• Multiple characters to understand • Figurative language	Blog Posts
Relationships in Nature	O	640L	Informational Text	• Multiple subtopics of larger topic • Prior knowledge needed to understand content	Description
Earth Environments	P	760L	Informational Text	• Content may be new to many students • Denser format of text	Description
What's for Dinner?	P	800L	Informational Text	• Some content-specific words defined in text • Denser format of text	Compare and Contrast
Slime in the Lake	P	750L	Science Fiction	• Challenging themes • Characters revealed by what they say and do	Chronological

Grade 3	UNIT 3	THEME: Heroes			
Title	Level	Lexile®	Genre	Text Elements	Text Structure
Camp Oneida	L	570L	Realistic Fiction	• Some new vocabulary • Situations outside typical experience	Chronological
After the Fire	L	530L	Realistic Fiction	• Some new vocabulary • Plot outside typical experience	Chronological
Inspiring Kids	L	690L	Biography	• Some new vocabulary explained in the text • Challenging multisyllable words	Compare and Contrast
How to Be a Hero	M	710L	Procedural	• Most content carried by text • Multisyllable words	Description
The Midnight Ride	M	710L	Historical Fiction	• Most content carried by text • Multisyllable words	Chronological
Animal Heroes	M	780L	Informational Text	• Most content carried by text • Multisyllable words	Compare and Contrast
The Hidden Treasure	N	690L	Mystery	• Multiple characters to understand • Sentences of varying length and complexity	Chronological
An Unlikely Friendship	N	680L	Fantasy	• Character's attributes shown in various ways • Sentences of varying length and complexity	Chronological
Community Heroes	N	790L	Informational Text	• Many three-syllable words • Some new vocabulary explained in the text	Compare and Contrast
The Kingdom That Never Laughed	O	570L	Fairytale	• Multiple characters to understand • Characters revealed by what they say and do	Chronological
Unforgettable Athletes	O	800L	Biography	• Multiple subtopics • Some content builds on prior knowledge	Compare and Contrast
Survivors	O	820L	Informational Text	• Multiple subtopics • Some content builds on prior knowledge	Compare and Contrast
Knight and Day	P	630L	Science Fiction	• Characters revealed by what they say and do • Extensive use of descriptive language	Chronological
Starboy	P	790L	Science Fiction	• Characters revealed by what they say and do • Suspense builds through plot events	Chronological
Eleanor Roosevelt	P	790L	Biography	• Content may be new to many students • Denser format of text	Description

Dig In!

Grade 3 — UNIT 4 — THEME: Events

Title	Level	Lexile®	Genre	Text Elements	Text Structure
Mysteries in Peru	M	610L	Mystery	• Most content carried by text • Multisyllable words offering decoding challenges	Chronological
Abandoned Cities	M	760L	Informational Text	• Most content carried by text • Multisyllable words	Compare and Contrast
People Who Changed U.S. History	M	790L	Narrative Nonfiction + Biography	• Most content carried by text • Additional information carried through captions	Compare and Contrast
The Journey Home	N	740L	Historical Fiction	• Character's attributes shown in various ways • Sentences of varying length and complexity	Chronological
Lali's Leaves	N	790L	Realistic Fiction	• Plot with numerous episodes • Content carried by text	Chronological
Daniel Boone	N	760L	Biography	• Some new vocabulary explained in the text • Maps with legends	Description
Creating Healthy Communities	O	820L	Informational Text	• Challenging multisyllable words • Multiple subtopics of a larger topic	Description
The Way Things Were	O	610L	Realistic Fiction	• Characters revealed by what they say and do • Minimal illustration	Description
Pizza Sauce From Mars	O	760L	Science Fiction	• Multiple characters to understand • Chapter titles	Chronological
Celebrating Martin Luther King Jr.	O	810L	Biography	• Some content builds on prior knowledge • Chapter titles, glossary, and index	Description
Gulliver in Lilliput	P	760L	Adaptation	• Characters revealed by what they say and do • Extensive use of descriptive language	Chronological
My New City	P	770L	Realistic Fiction	• Requires reader to take on diverse perspectives • Chapter titles	Chronological
Coming Together	P	820L	Informational Text (Biography)	• Variety of text features • Some new vocabulary explained in the text	Compare and Contrast
Scientific Breakthroughs	P	810L	Informational Text	• Content may be new to many students • Some new vocabulary explained in the text	Compare and Contrast
Have You Heard About Nome?	P	800L	Informational Text	• Content may be new to many students • Table of contents, glossary, and index	Description

Grade 3 — UNIT 5 — THEME: Solutions

Title	Level	Lexile®	Genre	Text Elements	Text Structure
In the Wild	N	600L	Realistic Fiction	• Plot with numerous episodes • Table of contents, chapter titles	Chronological
What Is It Made Of?	N	740L	Informational Text	• Presentation of multiple subtopics • Table of contents, glossary, and index	Compare and Contrast
Earth's Power	N	730L	Informational Text	• Presentation of multiple subtopics • Prefixes and suffixes	Compare and Contrast
Changing Habitats	N	810L	Informational Text	• Presentation of multiple subtopics • Some new vocabulary explained in the text	Description
Climbing Mountains	O	790L	Informational Text	• Multiple subtopics • Variety of text features	Description
The Hot-Dog Incident	O	640L	Realistic Fiction	• Characters revealed by what they say and do • Minimal illustration	Chronological
Tornado Tom	O	770L	Realistic Fiction	• Plot with numerous episodes • Story carried through text	Chronological
The Weighting Game	O	730L	Science Fiction	• Multiple characters to understand • Descriptive language	Chronological
Ice Ages	O	820L	Informational Text	• Challenging multisyllable words • Charts and diagrams	Description
The Australian Outback	P	800L	Informational Text	• Content may be new to many students • Maps and diagrams	Description
The Search for Jacob Pepper	P	670L	Realistic Fiction	• Characters revealed by what they say and do • Table of contents and chapter titles	Chronological
Diving with Monsters	P	730L	Realistic Fiction	• Characters revealed by what they say and do • Extensive use of descriptive language	Chronological
Plug Into the Sun	P	800L	Realistic Fiction	• Characters revealed by what they say and do • Extensive use of descriptive language	Chronological
Watching the Weather	P	810L	Informational Text	• Variety of text features • Some new vocabulary explained in the text	Description
Keeping Our Water Clean	P	820L	Informational Text	• Some new vocabulary explained in the text • Charts and diagrams	Description

Grade 4	UNIT 1	THEME: Networks			
Title	Level	Lexile®	Genre	Text Elements	Text Structure
Firefighting in the Sky	O	740L	Realistic Fiction	• Characters revealed by what they do, say, and think • Figurative language	Chronological
The Mongolian Medallion	O	770L	Historical Fiction	• Multisyllable proper nouns • Figurative language	Letters
Railroad Networks	P	920L	Informational Text	• Content may be new to many students • Content-specific words defined in text	Description
Landmarks of the World	P	920L	Narrative Nonfiction	• Content-specific words defined in text or glossary • Dense layout of text	Description
The Light at Jupiter Lake	Q	800L	Mystery	• Figurative language • Text with deeper meanings	Chronological
Homes in Early America	Q	890L	Narrative Nonfiction	• Many new vocabulary words • Words that offer decoding challenges	Description
No Place Like Home	R	920L	Narrative Nonfiction	• Many new vocabulary words • Words that offer decoding challenges	Description
Living on Earth	R	920L	Informational Text	• Words with complex spelling patterns • Many new vocabulary words	Description
Texas: A Living Land	R	930L	Informational Article	• Settings distant from some students' experiences • Words with complex spelling patterns	Description
Maui Snares the Sun	S	760L	Traditional Literature	• Meaning of new vocabulary derived from context • Extensive figurative language	Chronological
Geographic Regions	S	920L	Informational Text	• Meaning of new vocabulary derived from context • Dense layout of text	Compare and Contrast
The Landscape of Sports	S	920L	Narrative Nonfiction	• Settings distant from some students' experiences • Words that offer decoding challenges	Compare and Contrast
Why Would You Live There?	T	940L	Narrative Nonfiction	• Multiple topics and subcategories • Some words from languages other than English	Description
Keeping Nature in Balance	T	930L	Informational Text	• Multiple topics and subcategories • Many words with affixes	Description
Health and Home	T	930L	Informational Text	• Focus on human issues • Multiple topics and subcategories	Description

Grade 4	UNIT 2	THEME: Adaptations			
Title	Level	Lexile®	Genre	Text Elements	Text Structure
Living in Space	O	910L	Informational Text	• Many subtopics of a larger topic • Challenging multisyllable words	Description
Eat Up!	O	880L	Expository Text	• Many subtopics of a larger topic • Challenging multisyllable words	Description
Jellyfish	P	890L	Informational Text	• Topics beyond readers' personal experiences • Complex content-specific words	Description
Evergreen Valley	P	790L	Fantasy	• Dense text layout • Building of suspense through plot events	Chronological
The Urban Jungle	Q	830L	Informational Text	• Words that are seldom used in oral language • Glossary, index	Compare and Contrast
Where Am I? Amazing Natural Camouflage	Q	930L	Informational Text	• New vocabulary depends on glossary • Words seldom used in oral language	Description
Rain Forest Retreat	R	750L	Fantasy	• Figurative language • Setting distant from readers' experiences	Chronological
Wildfires	R	920L	Informational Text	• Words with complex spelling patterns • Many new vocabulary words	Description
Here Comes the Night	R	870L	Expository Text	• Settings distant from some students' experiences • Words with complex spelling patterns	Compare and Contrast
One Morning on Mars	S	830L	Science Fiction	• Minimal illustrations • Long stretches of descriptive language	Chronological
Invasive Species	S	940L	Expository Text	• Dense text layout • Glossary, index	Description
Plant and Animal Communication	S	930L	Expository Text	• Dense text layout • Glossary, index	Description
The Nightingale's Song	T	780L	Traditional Literature	• Minimal illustrations • Words from languages other than English	Chronological
Exploring Ecosystems	T	930L	Informational Text	• Multiple topics and subcategories • Many words with affixes	Description
Sleep	T	890L	Expository Text	• Focus on human issues • Multiple topics and subcategories	Description

Grade 4 — UNIT 3 — THEME: Diversity

Title	Level	Lexile®	Genre	Text Elements	Text Structure
Fool's Gold	O	780L	Realistic Fiction	• Characters revealed by what they do, say, and think • Figurative language	Chronological
From City to Island	O	740L	Realistic Fiction	• Characters revealed by what they do, say, and think • Figurative language	Chronological
The Sky's the Limit	P	920L	Biographies	• Content new to many students • Complex content-specific words	Compare and Contrast
Sports: Bringing People Together	P	930L	Informational Text	• Topics beyond readers' personal experiences • Dense text format	Description
Moves and Grooves	Q	870L	Informational Text	• Some new vocabulary depends on glossary • Meaning of new vocabulary derived from text	Compare and Contrast
Rosy's Journey	Q	790L	Traditional Literature	• Meaning of some new vocabulary derived from text • Text with deeper meaning	Chronological
The Unbreakable Code	R	750L	Historical Fiction	• Figurative language • Setting distant from readers' experiences	Chronological
Camporee	R	840L	Realistic Fiction	• Long passages of descriptive language • Meaning of some new vocabulary derived from text	Chronological
Working in Harmony	R	800L	Realistic Fiction	• Long passages of descriptive language • Meaning of some new vocabulary derived from text	Chronological
Fruitful Friendships	S	790L	Realistic Fiction	• Descriptive language • Figurative language	Chronological
One Nation, One People	S	880L	Historical Fiction	• Vocabulary meaning derived from context • Dense content and format	Stories within Stories
The Power of Words	S	910L	Informational Text	• Meaning of new vocabulary derived from context • Dense layout of text	Description
The Ruby Amulet	T	840L	Fantasy	• Wide range of sentence types • Complex fantasy elements	Chronological
A World of Games	T	930L	Expository Text	• Some words from languages other than English • Multiple topics and subcategories	Compare and Contrast
One World, Many Cultures	T	830L	Informational Text	• Some words from languages other than English • Multiple topics and subcategories	Description

Grade 4 — UNIT 4 — THEME: Impacts

Title	Level	Lexile®	Genre	Text Elements	Text Structure
How Anansi Got His Stories	P	760L	Traditional Literature	• Dense text layout • Multiple characters to understand	Chronological
Grandpa Bill's Tall Tales	P	760L	Traditional Literature	• Dense text layout • Multiple characters to understand	Chronological
Run Like the River	Q	760L	Historical Fiction	• Figurative language • Challenging themes	Chronological
The Earth Assignment	Q	760L	Science Fiction	• Meaning of some new vocabulary derived from text • Figurative language	Chronological
A Tale of Two Volcanoes	R	850L	Traditional Literature	• Figurative language • Setting distant from readers' experiences	Chronological
The Age of the Vikings	R	920L	Narrative Nonfiction	• Content may be new to many students • Words with complex spelling patterns	Description
Leaders of Change	R	890L	Informational Text	• Words with complex spelling patterns • Complex ideas on a variety of topics	Description
The Banquet	S	840L	Traditional Story	• Long stretches of descriptive language • Figurative language	Chronological
An Epic Tale	S	880L	Traditional Literature	• New vocabulary derived from context • Figurative language	Chronological
Striking a Chord	S	920L	Narrative Nonfiction	• Content appealing to preadolescents • Vocabulary words depend on context or glossary	Description
Enriching America	S	920L	Informational Text (Biographies)	• Meaning of new vocabulary derived from context • Dense layout of text	Description
Flash in the Pan	T	800L	Historical Fiction	• Wide range of sentence types • Words with affixes	Chronological
Great American Speeches	T	940L	Informational Text	• Wide range of sentence types • Multiple topics and subcategories	Compare and Contrast
The Simuteller's Last Tale	T	760L	Traditional Literature	• Wide range of sentence types • Words with affixes	Chronological
Stories of Storytellers	T	920L	Biography	• Wide range of sentence types • Multiple topics and subcategories	Compare and Contrast

Grade 4	UNIT 5	THEME: Features			
Title	**Level**	**Lexile®**	**Genre**	**Text Elements**	**Text Structure**
Challenge in the Rain Field	Q	740L	Myth	• Meaning of some new vocabulary derived from text • Figurative language	Chronological
Digging for Dinosaurs	Q	930L	Expository Text	• Some new vocabulary depends on glossary • Variety of text features	Description
Understanding the Universe	Q	910L	Biography	• Some new vocabulary depends on glossary • Diagrams	Compare and Contrast
Tales of Mother Earth	R	830L	Traditional Tales	• Figurative language • Minimal illustration	Chronological
The Water Cycle	R	890L	Expository Text + Procedure	• Words with complex spelling patterns • Variety of text features	Description
Patterns in Nature	R	900L	Informational Text + Procedure	• Some new vocabulary defined in text • Diagrams	Description
Earth's Natural Treasures	R	910L	Informational Text	• Some new vocabulary defined in text • Diagrams	Description
Adventure in Antarctica	S	790L	Realistic Fiction	• Long stretches of descriptive language • Chapter titles	Chronological
Force and Energy	S	910L	Informational Text	• Meaning of new vocabulary derived from context • Variety of text features	Description
Exploring Our World	S	930L	Informational Text	• Maps and legends, diagrams • Some new vocabulary defined in text	Description
The Dirt on Soil	S	920L	Informational Text	• Meaning of new vocabulary derived from context • Graphs and diagrams	Description
How Weather Works	T	920L	Expository Text	• Wide range of sentence types • Charts and diagrams	Description
Trouble on Zeplin 5	T	800L	Science Fiction	• Wide range of sentence types • Words with affixes	Chronological
Marvels and Mysteries of Nature	T	830L	Informational Text	• Wide range of sentence types • Maps and legends	Description
Accidental Discoveries	T	920L	Narrative Nonfiction	• Multiple subtopics • Maps and legends	Description

Grade 5	UNIT 1	THEME: Journeys			
Title	**Level**	**Lexile®**	**Genre**	**Text Elements**	**Text Structure**
Travel the World	S	880L	Narrative Nonfiction	• Variety of spelling patterns • New vocabulary that depends on glossary	Compare and Contrast
Legendary European Explorers	S	970L	Informational Text	• Many words with affixes • Some new vocabulary dependent on glossary	Compare and Contrast
Unexpected Summer	S	840L	Realistic Fiction	• Long stretches of descriptive language • Figurative language	Chronological
The City of Machu Picchu	T	990L	Informational Text	• Affixes • Words from languages other than English	Description
Interesting Lives, Interesting Journeys	T	980L	Biography	• Multiple topics and subcategories • Words from languages other than English	Compare and Contrast
Passport to Peru	T	910L	Realistic Fiction	• Wide range of sentence types • Words from languages other than English	Chronological
Journey to the New World	U	1000L	Informational Text	• Content may be new to many students • Complex graphics	Description
Inspiring Journeys	U	860L	Short Stories	• Content may be new to many students • Minimal illustration	Stories within Stories
Incredible Journeys	U	930L	Narrative Nonfiction	• Variety of graphics • Content may be new to many students	Compare and Contrast
Lewis and Clark: Westward Exploration	V	1010L	Informational Text	• Content may be new to many students • Words from languages other than English	Description
Challenger Deep	V	840L	Science Fiction	• Content may be new to many students • Words used figuratively	Chronological
Discovering the Ancient Maya	V	980L	Expository Text	• Variety of graphics • Content may be new to many students	Description
The Vole of RektoFor	W	840L	Animal Fantasy	• Fantasy incorporating quest motif • Full range of literary devices	Chronological
Flight	W	980L	Informational Text	• Words from languages other than English • Archaic words	Description
Matthew Henson: Arctic Explorer	W	1010L	Biography	• Words from languages other than English • Photographs with captions	Description

Dig In!

Grade 5	UNIT 2	THEME: Observations			
Title	Level	Lexile®	Genre	Text Elements	Text Structure
The Horse of Seven Colors	S	830L	Traditional Literature	• Descriptive language • Figurative language	Chronological
Eating Well	S	970L	Informational Text	• Dense content and format • Some new words depend on glossary	Description
Newearth	S	900L	Science Fiction	• Descriptive language • Figurative language	Chronological
Smalled	T	830L	Fantasy	• Minimal illustration • Wide range of sentence types	Chronological
Hatching a Surprise	T	940L	Realistic Fiction	• Minimal illustration • Wide range of sentence types	Chronological
An Icelandic Adventure	T	850L	Realistic Fiction	• Minimal illustration • Wide range of sentence types	Chronological
Making Observations	U	950L	Informational Text	• Extensive use of text boxes • Diagrams	Description
A System of Life	U	970L	Informational Text	• Variety of graphics • Multisyllable words	Description
Trapped in Carnivorous Plants	U	950L	Expository Text	• Variety of graphics • Multisyllable words	Description
Instruments of Science	V	1000L	Expository Text	• Extensive use of domain-specific vocabulary • Photographs with captions	Description
Surprise! Great Accidental Inventions	V	990L	Expository Text (Biography)	• Domain-specific vocabulary • Photographs with captions	Description
An Eye on Ecosystems	V	950L	Informational Text	• Photographs with captions • Maps, legends, and diagrams	Description
Fit for Survival	W	1000L	Informational Text	• Extensive use of text boxes • Decoding challenges	Description
Science in the Wild	W	980L	Narrative Nonfiction	• Some information carried through photo captions • Decoding challenges	Description
Animal Behaviors	W	990L	Expository Text	• Content-specific words defined in text or glossary • Words that offer decoding challenges	Description

Grade 5	UNIT 3	THEME: Reflections			
Title	Level	Lexile®	Genre	Text Elements	Text Structure
The New Neighbor	S	840L	Science Fiction	• Complex ideas • Long stretches of descriptive language	Chronological
Food From Around the World	S	980L	Expository Text	• Dense content and format • Some new words depend on glossary	Compare and Contrast
Stories From Turtle Island	S	840L	Traditional Literature	• Long stretches of descriptive language • Figurative language	Chronological
The International Fair	T	860L	Realistic Fiction	• Many words with prefixes and suffixes • Minimal illustration	Chronological
My Village School	T	860L	Realistic Fiction	• Range of sentence types • Words from languages other than English	Chronological
Missing!	T	840L	Mystery	• Themes about issues of preadolescents • Wide range of sentence types	Chronological
Sky Surfers	U	860L	Fantasy	• Requires inference to understand why characters change • Content appealing to preadolescents	Chronological
Social Media	U	970L	Expository Text	• Content appealing to preadolescents • Multisyllable words requiring attention to roots	Description
From Peewee to Pro	U	970L	Informational Text	• Content appealing to preadolescents • Some words from languages other than English	Compare and Contrast
Women's Rights	U	1000L	Informational Text	• Content appealing to preadolescents • Vocabulary words depend on context or glossary	Description
Circle of Friends	V	870L	Realistic Fiction	• Figurative language • Theme presents social issues	Chronological
Trailhead	V	900L	Realistic Fiction	• Figurative language • Changes of setting	Chronological
Cross-Cultural Kids	V	980L	Informational Text	• Variety of text features • Societal themes	Description
In the Spotlight	W	1000L	Informational Text	• Content-specific words defined in text or glossary • Words that offer decoding challenges	Compare and Contrast
The Mirror of Matsuyama	W	980L	Traditional Literature	• Minimal illustration • Figurative language	Chronological
Tell Me a Story	W	970L	Expository Text	• Variety of text boxes • Photographs with captions	Compare and Contrast

Grade 5	UNIT 4	THEME: Liberty			
Title	Level	Lexile®	Genre	Text Elements	Text Structure
Something in the Air	T	840L	Historical Fiction	• Wide range of sentence types • Minimal illustration	Chronological
Akoko and Abruburo	T	900L	Traditional Literature	• Wide range of sentence types • Minimal illustration	Chronological
The World Beneath the Waves	T	870L	Historical Fiction	• Wide range of sentence types • Minimal illustration	Chronological
The Cabin	U	850L	Historical Fiction	• Figurative language • Themes build social awareness	Chronological
Reflections in Glass Town	U	880L	Historical Fiction	• Figurative language • Inference required to understand characters	Chronological
Aim for the Stars	U	840L	Realistic Fiction	• Figurative language • Minimal illustration	Chronological
Pathways to Freedom	V	1000L	Narrative Nonfiction	• Variety of text features • Societal themes	Description
A Slimy Situation	V	830L	Mystery	• Figurative language • Changes of setting	Chronological
To Tell the Truth	V	840L	Historical Fiction	• Figurative language • Theme presents social issues	Chronological
Road to Freedom	V	950L	Informational Text	• Variety of text features • Vocabulary words depend on context or glossary	Description
Welcome, Citizen	W	850L	Science Fiction	• Themes build social awareness • Themes that evoke multiple interpretations	Chronological
Power of the People	W	990L	Expository Text	• Themes build social awareness • Content-specific words defined in text or glossary	Compare and Contrast
Freedom and Technology	W	980L	Informational Text	• Themes build social awareness • Content-specific words defined in text or glossary	Description
A Child's Rights	W	960L	Report	• Variety of text features • Vocabulary words depend on context or glossary	Description

Grade 5	UNIT 5	THEME: Systems			
Title	Level	Lexile®	Genre	Text Elements	Text Structure
Flood!	U	850L	Realistic Fiction	• Figurative language • Content may be new to some students	Chronological
The Changing Earth	U	1000L	Informational Text	• Diagrams and charts • Vocabulary words depend on context or glossary	Description
Tropical Rain Forests	U	870L	Informational Text	• Maps and diagrams • Multiple subtopics presented	Description
Earth: The Ripple Effect	U	960L	Expository Text	• Maps and diagrams • Multiple subtopics presented	Compare and Contrast
Ocean Forces	V	990L	Informational Text	• Maps and diagrams • New vocabulary depends on context or glossary	Description
The Spammer	V	870L	Science Fiction	• Figurative language • Theme presents social issues	Chronological
Making Mountains	V	970L	Fantasy	• Figurative language • Changes of setting	Chronological
Mission to the Stars	V	990L	Informational Text	• Variety of text features • New vocabulary depends on context or glossary	Description
Earth's Changing Landscape	V	850L	Expository Text	• Variety of text features • Presents multiple subtopics	Description
The Time Travelers	W	920L	Science Fiction	• Themes build social awareness • Figurative language	Chronological
Protecting Our Planet	W	1000L	Informational Text	• Themes build social awareness • Content-specific words defined in text or glossary	Compare and Contrast
Earth's Fury	W	1000L	Informational Text	• Maps and diagrams • Multiple subtopics presented	Compare and Contrast
Power Up!	W	1000L	Expository Text with Procedure	• Timelines and diagrams • Content-specific words defined in text or glossary	Compare and Contrast
How Do We Feed the World?	W	980L	Informational Text	• Themes build social awareness • Content-specific words defined in text or glossary	Description
Saving the Great Lakes	W	1000L	Informational Text	• Maps and diagrams • Multiple subtopics presented	Description

How can I promote language development through small group conversations?

Build Engagement

All the skills in the world won't be useful if students don't enjoy reading and find the experience useful and enjoyable. An engaged reader is much more likely to become a good and lifelong reader. Building engagement, focus, and stamina when reading will help develop powerful, curious readers. Engage students in talking about reading.

Describe the perfect spot for reading.

What books have you chosen to read? Why did you select them?

When your mind wanders, where will you start to reread?

You seem distracted. What will help you focus on what you are reading?

How many pages do you plan to read today? What is your goal?

Based on what you know about this author/topic, what do you think will happen next?

What questions have come to you as you read this book?

How does this writer's style compare to the style of the writer of the last book?

What are some of the books you have loved? What do they have in common?

How are you keeping track of your reading? Did you include your time in your reading log?

Conferring

Talking with students about what they are reading and writing can be a teacher's best detective tool. As discussed in Chapter 2, conferring should be purposeful and systematic.

Conferring Do's	Conferring Don'ts
Focus on learning about a student's strengths and build upon them.	Focus only on what a student missed or what deficiencies are uncovered.
Encourage students to talk about what they have done, and to bring writing samples, favorites readings, and reading logs to share.	Do most of the talking and make it a stressful experience for the student.
End the time with agreed upon goals and next steps. Record your notes.	Provide vague goals with little closure.

English Language Learners

Many students who are in the process of acquiring English are more willing to participate in small group activities because the smaller group is less intimidating than the whole class. The teacher can also focus attention on individual language strengths and make modifications as needed.

English Language Learners benefit from:

- Instruction and practice that take into account a student's level of language acquisition

- The use of visual supports

- Time spent listening to English being spoken and time spent speaking English

- Encouragement for, and awareness of the challenges of, learning a new language

- Adjustments to the difficulty of the language used to present information rather than reducing the rigor of the content

How can I use writing to build on what students have read?

Purpose

Writing about what students have read, or the genre they have read, provides them with a well-crafted model to use for their own writing and a chance to reflect on, or give an opinion about, what they have read. Going back into previously read material encourages students to read more deeply and notice the decisions an author makes in the stages of their writing.

Procedures

Minilesson: Minilessons should be focused. Provide instruction about the topic, the writing genre, a writing principle, or a writing convention. Connect the minilesson to the text students have read.

Writing and Conferring: As students work through the writing process, take opportunities for one-to-one or small group conferencing to address strengths or areas for growth.

Sharing: Proud writers look forward to sharing what they have created. Schedule a time and venue for this to be part of the process. Vary the ways students share their work throughout the year.

Question: How can I make my minilesson more effective?

Answer: Decide on the focus of the minilesson. Rather than trying to address or demonstrate every issue that will come up when writing, select one area as the focus of that minilesson. You can select a different focus for the next day. Work with students to find examples of the minilesson focus within the text they are reading.

Question: What types of prompts or questions are most useful when conferring with students about their writing?

Answer: It works best to keep prompts short and focused on the area you taught in the minilesson. If the minilesson is about writing clear opening sentences, this is not the best time to divert attention to punctuating compound sentences.

- Try specific compliments: e.g., "That opening grabs my attention because of the words 'crept toward' in the first sentence."

- Try a specific suggestion: e.g., "You said 'what happened first'. Try thinking of words that would excite or intrigue the reader."

- Try an incomplete sentence or sentence starter: e.g., "At first I . . . After that . . . At last . . ."

Question: Other than just posting their writing on the bulletin board, how can I have students show off their writing?

Answer: Posting the work for all to see is certainly one way to have students share their work. Some other options would be:

- Reading to another class
- Performing the work as a short play
- Using the writing as the foundation for a debate
- Reading to a partner
- Putting the work in a Brag Book to save
- Making a video or audio recording of students reading their work
- Creating a class website or blog to share their writing

Habits of Good Readers

Fiction and Nonfiction

SKILLS: *Visualizing, Monitoring for Meaning*

Strategy: **Reading and Thinking**

Think Aloud:

> As I read, I make notes. The notes help me learn new words, connect ideas, and write down questions I have. As I read, I also think about how to find clues to a word's meaning, how ideas go together, and how to clarify the part of the text I don't understand. I'm always thinking about what I'm reading as I read.

Reading and Thinking

READ: Circle new and interesting words.

THINK: Look for clues about the words.

READ: Underline important ideas.

THINK: Put the ideas together.

READ: Write questions.

THINK: Look for answers in the text.

Coaching Conversations

- Tell me what you know about this circled word.
- What is the connection between these ideas?
- How can you find the answer to this question?

Focus and Stamina

SKILLS: *Retelling, Monitoring for Meaning, Questioning*

Strategy: **Keep a Reading Log**

Think Aloud:

> " I can set reading goals for myself. This helps me to build my reading stamina. I keep a log of my reading. I write the date and the title of my book. Then I decide how many pages I want to read in my book that day. I mark that place in my book. Finally, after I've finished reading, I can see if I met my goal. "

Keep a Reading Log

Date: October 30

Title of Book:
The Stories Julian Tells

My Reading Goals:
I want to read **32** pages today.
I read **35** pages today.

My Favorite Part:
I like the part where he
tricks his brother.

Coaching Conversations

- How many pages have you been reading?
- What is your reading goal for today?
- How did you do in reaching your reading goal?

Listening and Speaking

GENRE: Fiction and Nonfiction

SKILLS: *Following Rules, Focusing, Engaging*

Strategy: ## Rules for Classroom Conversations

Think Aloud:

> The first rule for classroom conversation is to be respectful. These rules help me to listen and speak carefully. If I didn't listen, I would miss important information. If I didn't speak clearly or stay on topic, then it would be hard for others to understand me. We take turns speaking, and we ask and answer questions.

Rules for Classroom Conversations

Be respectful!
Listen carefully.
Speak when it's your turn.
Look at others when you speak.
Speak clearly.
Stay on the topic.
Ask and answer questions.

Coaching Conversations

- What is one classroom rule for speaking?
- What is one classroom rule for listening?
- Why are classroom rules important?

SKILLS: *Focusing, Asking Questions, Elaborating, Sequencing*

Strategy: **Working with Others**

Think Aloud:

> George and I were working together. Every time George said something, I would get really excited and interrupt him. He has such good ideas. He got very frustrated because he couldn't finish sharing his ideas. George reminded me of the rules for working together. He was right! I apologized. Then I really tried to listen actively and waited for my turn to speak.

Working with Others

Listen actively.

Take turns.

Speak clearly.

Speak in complete sentences.

Ask questions.

Encourage everyone to speak.

Coaching Conversations

- How do you know when it's your turn to speak?
- What can you add to what was said?
- How can you encourage others to share their ideas?

Word Study

SKILLS: *Decoding, Monitoring for Meaning, Understanding How Words Work*

Strategy: **Adding Endings**

Think Aloud:

" You can add endings to words, such as *-ing*, *-ed*, *-es*, and *-able*. Sometimes, you need to change the spelling of the base word. When you add *-ing* or *-ed* to some words, you double the ending consonant: *hop, hopping, hopped.* When you add *-es*, you change the final *y* to an *i*: *baby, babies.* When you add *-able*, you might have to drop the final *e*: *usable.* "

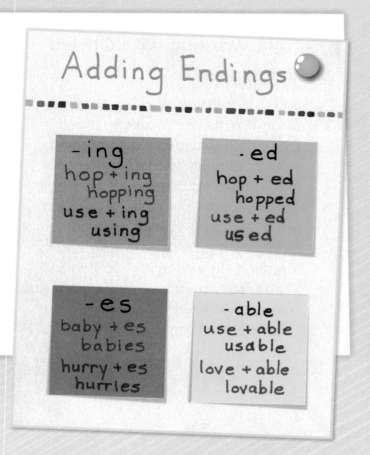

Adding Endings

-ing
hop + ing
hopping
use + ing
using

-ed
hop + ed
hopped
use + ed
used

-es
baby + es
babies
hurry + es
hurries

-able
use + able
usable
love + able
lovable

Coaching Conversations

- What happens when you add *-ing* to the word *drop*?
- What happens to the final *e* when you add *-ed*?
- How do you spell the word *babies*?

GENRE: Fiction and Nonfiction

SKILLS: *Intonation, Expression, Monitoring for Meaning*

Strategy: **Checking for Accuracy**

Think Aloud:

" I just read this sentence from a book about George Washington: "George Washington tires to win the war." Something doesn't sound or look right. I said the word *tires*. Is *tires* right? The word on the page begins with the letters *t-r*. *Tires* begins with *t-i*. Also, you don't "tire" to do something. You "try" to do something. I think the word should be *tries*. "

Checking for Accuracy

Does it look right?

Does it sound right?

Does it make sense?

What other word would make more sense?

Coaching Conversations

- Does the word look right? Tell why or why not.
- Does the word sound right? Tell why or why not.
- Does the word make sense? Tell why or why not.

Comprehension

SKILLS: *Comparing and Contrasting, Making Connections, Drawing Conclusions*

Strategy: **Comparing and Contrasting Settings**

Think Aloud:

> The myth "Fire" is set at the beginning of the world. Bear and his people come to a great forest. "What We Plant, We Will Eat" is a folktale set long ago on a small farm in Korea. Comparing and contrasting the settings will help me understand how myths and folktales are alike and different. I can use words to help me compare—*also, both*—and contrast—*but, however*.

Comparing and Contrasting Settings

How are the settings alike?	How are the settings different?
Where? The myth and the folktale are both set in _____.	Where? The myth is set in _____, but the folktale is set in _____.
When? The myth takes place in _____. The folktale also takes place in _____.	When? The myth takes place in _____. However, the folktale takes place in _____.

Coaching Conversations

- Which story is a myth? Which is a folktale?
- What is the setting of this myth/folktale?
- Which story was probably told first? Why do you think so?

SKILLS: *Inferring, Interpreting*

Strategy: **Point of View**

Think Aloud:

> " The main character in this myth is the goddess Athena. She's not the narrator. She's not telling the story. Someone outside the story is telling it. I know this because the narrator uses the pronouns *she*, *he*, *they*, *her*, *him*, and *them* to tell what's happening and who's speaking. The story is told from the third-person point of view. "

Point of View
Who's telling this story?

First Person: I am!	Third Person: She is!
Look for these Pronouns: I, me, my	Look for these pronouns: She, he, her, him
The speaker or narrator is *inside* the story.	The speaker or narrator is *outside* the story.

Coaching Conversations

- Who is telling this story?
- Which pronouns do you see in the story?
- Is the narrator inside or outside the story? How do you know?

GENRE: Fiction and Nonfiction

SKILLS: *Determining Importance, Summarizing, Locating Information*

Strategy: **Make Inferences**

Think Aloud:

> Sometimes, an author doesn't say something directly in a text. Readers need to infer what the author wants them to know. To infer, I read carefully. I look for clues in the text. I look for details, including facts and examples. I think of what I know about the topic. Then I can put together that information to infer meaning.

Make Inferences

To infer, you add.

Clues in the text + What I know

Look for <u>details</u>.   Think of

Find <u>facts</u> and   what you know

<u>examples</u>.   about the topic.

Coaching Conversations

- What inference can you make about this part of the text?
- Which clues in the text support your inference?
- How did you use what you know to infer that?

Comprehension

SKILLS: *Determining Importance, Summarizing*

Strategy: **Using Text Features**

Think Aloud:

" I'm reading about needs and wants in my social studies textbook. When I want to locate information quickly, I use text features. I look for words in bold print. Those words appear in the glossary in the back of the book, so I can look up their meanings. Words in italics often have definitions of those words nearby. I also scan for key words about the topic. "

Using Text Features

Use text features to find information.

Look for:
➡ Words in Bold Print:
Food and water are **needs**.
➡ Words in Italics:
The word *want* means
"something you wish for."
➡ Key Words About the Topic:
People can spend or save for a want.

Coaching Conversations

- Which words are in bold print?
- Why is this word in italics?
- Show me the key words in this sentence.

Figurative Language

SKILLS: *Understanding How Words Work, Visualizing, Analyzing*

Strategy: ## That's an Exaggeration!

Think Aloud:

> This folktale is a tall tale about Sally Ann Thunder Ann Whirlwind. I can tell it's a tall tale because the writer uses hyperboles, or exaggeration, to describe Sally Ann. She is "tougher than a grumpy bear." She is "sweeter than honey." She is also "faster than a wildcat with its tail on fire." The writer exaggerates Sally Ann's character traits. The hyperbole keeps me interested in the story.

That's an Exaggeration!

Hyperbole is an **exaggerated** statement.

I'm really tired.
I'm so tired, I could sleep for a year.

Sam is hungry.
Sam is so hungry, he could eat a horse.

The store has a lot of toys.
The store has millions of toys.

Coaching Conversations

- How does the author describe the character?
- Is this a hyperbole? How do you know?
- Read this hyperbole. What do you see in your mind?

Vocabulary

SKILLS: *Categorizing, Recognizing Words, Making Meaning*

Strategy: **Use Context Clues**

Think Aloud:

> I'm not sure what the word *raise* means in this sentence: "He got a raise." I'll look for clues around the word. The sentence before tells where Nam works. The sentence after says Nam makes more money because of the raise. *Raise* can be a verb, but in this sentence, it's used as a noun. If I put it all together, I think *raise* means that Nam is getting more money at work.

Use Context Clues

"Nam <u>works</u> at the pet store. He got a [raise.] Now he <u>makes more money</u>."

- Look for clues around the word.
- Think about the part of speech.
- Use what you know.
- Figure out the word's meaning.

Coaching Conversations

- Which word is unfamiliar?
- How is the word used in this sentence?
- What clues do you see before or after the word?

SKILLS: *Categorizing, Monitoring for Meaning, Activating Prior Knowledge*

Strategy: **Autobiography or Biography?**

Think Aloud:

" I'm reading a biography of George Washington Carver called *The Little Plant Doctor*. It's by Jean Marzollo. She uses the third person, *he*. On the Internet, I saw the book *George Washington Carver, In His Own Words*. Carver wrote that book himself. It's an autobiography. The Greek word *auto* means "self." In it, Carver uses the first person, *I*. "

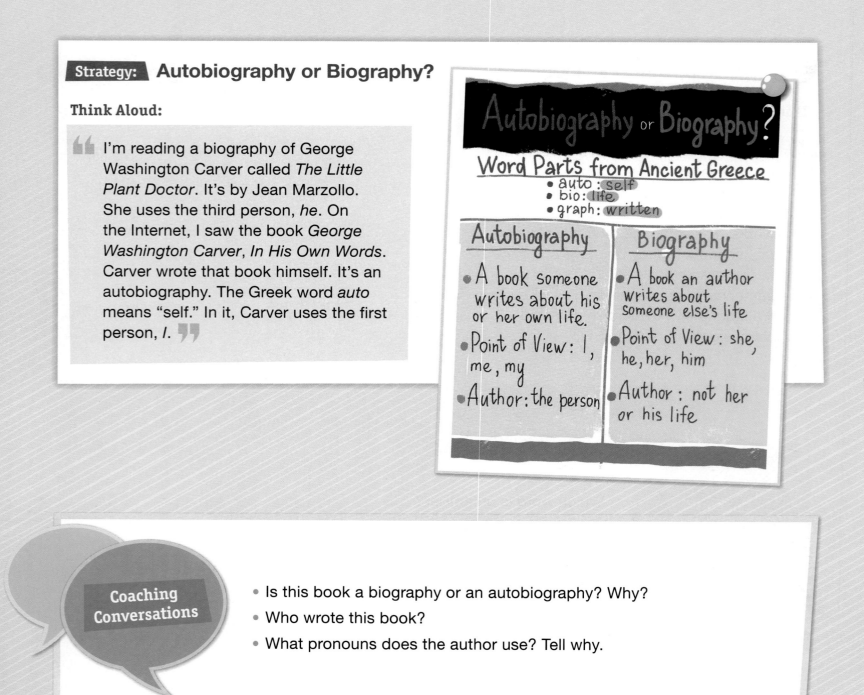

Autobiography or Biography?

Word Parts from Ancient Greece
- auto: self
- bio: life
- graph: written

Autobiography	Biography
• A book someone writes about his or her own life.	• A book an author writes about someone else's life
• Point of View: I, me, my	• Point of View: she, he, her, him
• Author: the person	• Author: not her or his life

Coaching Conversations

- Is this book a biography or an autobiography? Why?
- Who wrote this book?
- What pronouns does the author use? Tell why.

SKILLS: *Identifying Cause and Effect, Analyzing, Connecting Ideas*

Strategy: **Cause and Effect in Nonfiction**

Think Aloud:

> Good readers ask questions when they read nonfiction, too. They ask, "What happened?" and "Why did that happen?" In a science text, a writer might use a cause-and-effect text structure to connect ideas. In a social studies text, a writer might use a cause-and-effect text structure to show how events are connected.

Cause and Effect in Nonfiction

To find the cause, ask: Why did it happen?

To find the effect, ask: What happened?

The effect often appears first.

Look for key words: since, if, then, this caused.

Gold was discovered in California. This caused many Americans to go there.

Coaching Conversations

- What caused it to happen?
- What was the effect of what happened?
- How are these events/ideas connected?

Preparing to Write

SKILLS: *Reflecting, Considering Purpose, Taking Notes*

Strategy: Writing Informational Text

Think Aloud:

> I'm planning an informational composition about spiders. That means I'll write a few paragraphs about spiders. I start my plan with a topic sentence that tells what my writing will be about. Then I list evidence from my research. Each fact or detail supports the topic sentence. Finally, I plan my conclusion. I'll restate the topic sentence in a different way.

Writing Informational Text

Title All About Spiders

Topic Sentence Main Idea

There are a lot of things you can learn about spiders.

Supporting Sentences Facts and Details

1. Spiders have two body parts.
2. Spiders have eight legs.
3. Spiders have up to eight eyes.
4. Not all spiders spin webs.

Conclusion Restate the topic sentence.

You can learn many things about spiders!

Coaching Conversations

- What is the topic you're writing about?
- Which facts support your topic sentence?
- How can you use your topic sentence to end your informational text?

SKILLS: *Sequencing, Developing Ideas, Making Connections*

Strategy: **Sequence**

Think Aloud:

> I just read the end of the story I wrote. I did a good job of describing the character and setting. I introduced a problem for the character to solve. I got so interested in describing what the character looks like that I forgot to show how the character feels and changes—and how she solves her problem! I need to focus on developing the plot and sequence of events.

Sequence

Beginning:
Introduce the characters and setting. Is there a problem? Introduce it.

Middle:
What happens to the characters? Why does this event happen? How does this change the characters?

End:
How is the problem solved? How do the characters feel now?

Coaching Conversations

- What happens at the beginning of your story?
- What happens to the character?
- How does the character change?

GENRE: Fiction and Nonfiction

SKILLS: *Visualizing, Focusing, Questioning, Revising*

Strategy: **Sharing Drafts**

Think Aloud:

" I like Hannah's poem about horses. I could "see" what the horses looked like and how they moved as they ran. She uses some fun rhymes, too, like *mane* and *grain*. I didn't understand the last line of the poem, though. I'm not sure where the horses went. Maybe Hannah could add one or two lines to the poem to explain that more clearly. "

Sharing Drafts

Read. Think. Share.

1. Read or listen carefully.
2. Think.
   - What do you like about the draft?
   - What questions do you have?
   - How could the draft be even better?
   - How can you help the writer?
3. Share your ideas. Be respectful.

Coaching Conversations

- What do you like best about this draft?
- What specific feedback can you give?
- Think about what you want to say. Are you ready?

Word Choice in Writing

SKILLS: *Questioning, Visualizing, Elaborating, Revising*

Strategy: **Adding Support**

Think Aloud:

> I know I need to support my main idea with details when I write an informative text. When I write a persuasive text, I need to support my opinion with details, too. I wrote an informative text about bicycles. It is about how bicycles have changed. I am making sure each detail supports my main idea. If a detail doesn't support the main idea, I need to take it out.

Adding Support	Y	N
Does this fact support my opinion?		
Does this reason support my opinion?		
Does this fact support the main idea?		
Does this example support the main idea?		

Coaching Conversations

- What is your main idea/opinion?
- How does this detail support your main idea/opinion?
- What other fact or example could you use?

Grammar Conventions

GENRE: Fiction and Nonfiction

SKILLS: *Understanding How Words Work, Analyzing, Choosing Words*

Strategy: Build a Compound Sentence

Think Aloud:

> A compound sentence is two simple sentences joined together. Tiny words called coordinating conjunctions join the simple sentences. First, you write a simple sentence. Then, instead of a period, you use a comma. Next, you put the coordinating conjunction that makes sense in the sentence. Finally, you write the next simple sentence and end it with a period.

Build a Compound Sentence

Coordinating Conjunctions
and   but   or   so   yet   nor

1. Write a simple sentence.
2. Use a comma instead of a period.
3. Add a coordinating conjunction.
4. Write a simple sentence.
5. End with a period.

Kiko likes carrots, so she eats them every day.

Coaching Conversations

- Explain how to write a compound sentence.
- Point out the subjects/verbs in this sentence.
- Which coordinating conjunction could you use to join these sentences?

Research and Media Literacy

SKILLS: *Brainstorming, Questioning, Analyzing*

Strategy: **Taking Notes**

Think Aloud:

" I'm researching why dogs wag their tails. Taking notes will help me remember all the evidence I find. First, I write down information about my source. It could be a book, magazine, or web page. Then I write down all the important evidence I find from that source. I include key words and definitions, key details, and any questions I have. Then I can sort my evidence into groups. "

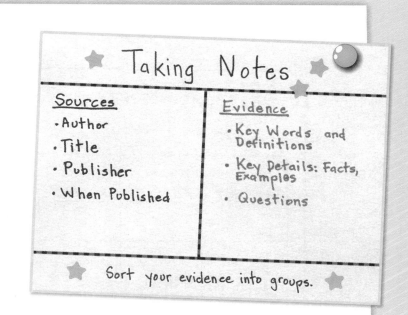

Taking Notes

Sources
- Author
- Title
- Publisher
- When Published

Evidence
- Key Words and Definitions
- Key Details: Facts, Examples
- Questions

★ Sort your evidence into groups. ★

Coaching Conversations

- What source are you using?
- Why is this piece of evidence important?
- What groups do you want to use for sorting your evidence?

Additional Anchor Charts for Reading and Writing

Use anchor charts such as these at any point to reinforce or refresh skills.

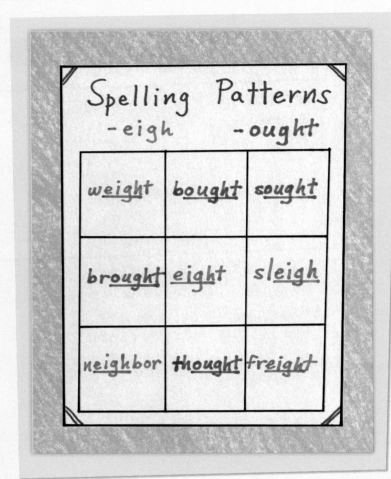

Spelling Patterns
-eigh   -ought

weight	bought	sought
brought	eight	sleigh
neighbor	thought	freight

Synonyms & Antonyms

Synonyms: Same	Antonyms: Opposite
yell, shout	yell, whisper
mad, angry	mad, happy
sick, ill	sick, healthy
give, present	give, take
close, shut	close, open
scared, afraid	scared, brave
friend, pal	friend, enemy
quiet, silent	quiet, loud
old, ancient	old, young

Additional Anchor Charts for Reading and Writing

Different Kinds of Poems

★ <u>Rhyming</u> <u>poems</u> have rhymes.

★ <u>Narrative</u> <u>poems</u> tell stories.

★ <u>Descriptive</u> <u>poems</u> use words to describe people, places, or things.

★ <u>Humorous</u> <u>poems</u> make readers laugh.

★ <u>Free</u> <u>verse</u> <u>poems</u> don't rhyme.

APOSTROPHES
- - - - - - - - - - - - - - - - - - -

An apostrophe (')

✱ is a punctuation mark.

✱ takes the place of a letter or letters in a word, forms a contraction: cannot, **can't**.

✱ shows ownership: **Max's** car.

Examples:

The **boy's** shirt is dirty.

It's snowing outside now.

The **teacher's** room is full.

She **won't** get there in time.

Additional Anchor Charts for Reading

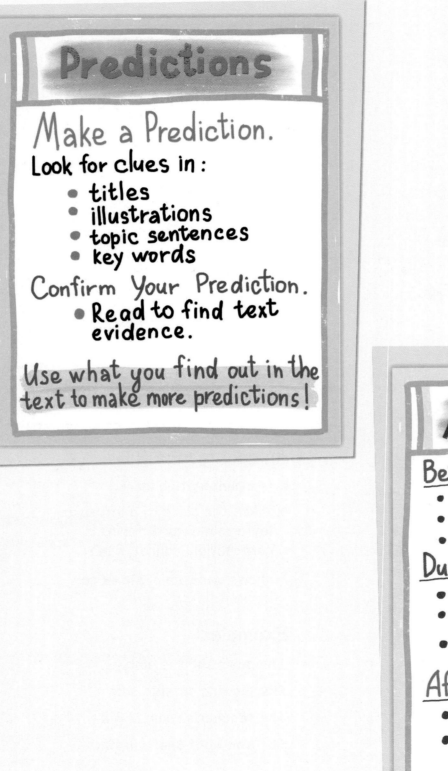

Predictions

Make a Prediction.
Look for clues in :
- titles
- illustrations
- topic sentences
- key words

Confirm Your Prediction.
- Read to find text evidence.

Use what you find out in the text to make more predictions!

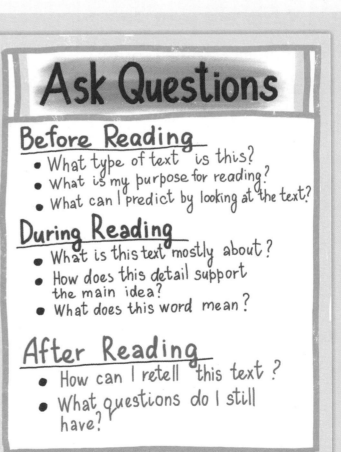

Ask Questions

Before Reading
- What type of text is this?
- What is my purpose for reading?
- What can I predict by looking at the text?

During Reading
- What is this text mostly about?
- How does this detail support the main idea?
- What does this word mean?

After Reading
- How can I retell this text?
- What questions do I still have?

Additional Anchor Charts for Writing

USE YOUR SENSES!

Help your readers

smell   see   hear   taste   feel

the details in your story or poem.

The frog makes a loud sound and then eats the fly.

Add details:
What does the frog look like?
What does the frog sound like?
Where are the frog and the fly?
What does that space smell like?
What does the fly taste like?

Persuade Me!
Convince Me!

State Your Opinion:
- What do you think?
- What do you want me to do?
(Be clear!)

Support Your Opinion:
- Why do you think that?
- Why should I do that?
(Use facts and details!)

Dig In!

for Reading

PURPOSE: Engage Readers

- What methods do you use to stay focused when you read?
- What do you look for when choosing a book that you think you'll enjoy?
- How long do you think you can read in one sitting?
- How does this book compare to the last book you read?

PURPOSE: Focus on Words

- Does that word make sense here?
- What other word could the author have used?
- What new words can you name with that same prefix/ending/root word?
- What do you do when you come to a word you don't know?

PURPOSE: Build Fluency

- How can you make your voice sound like a different character in the story?
- What do you look for to tell you when to stop or pause when reading?
- How would an expert on the topic read this?
- How does your voice change when you ask a question?
- What do you do when you see quotation marks?

PURPOSE: Check Comprehension

- How does the setting influence the characters? How might the story change if it happened in a different place or time?
- How do the captions help you understand the picture?
- What can you tell about this book by just reading the first page?
- What was the biggest change that happened in this story?
- What is something you learned from this book that you think most people don't know?

More Coaching Conversation Prompts **for Writing**

PURPOSE: Generate Ideas

- What picture do you want the readers to have in their minds as they read this?

- How are the characters in your story going to be different from each other?

- What is a big problem to be solved in your story?

- What facts do you want people to learn from what you will write?

- What position are you going to take on this topic?

PURPOSE: Using Drawings or Images

- What picture would help tell this part of the story without giving away too much?

- How could the pictures help show what has changed?

- What diagrams or charts would make this content clearer?

- How could you use captions or callouts to help the reader?

PURPOSE: Focus and Audience

- Who is going to be the most important person reading this?

- Where have you read a model for this type of writing?

- What could be left out?

- Does everything fit together? How do you know?

PURPOSE: Clarification and Elaboration

- If readers know nothing about the topic, what could you include to help them?

- If a person made this into a movie, what additional details would they need?

- What other details can you add to make the characters or setting come alive?

- Are there words that should be defined because they might be new to some readers?

What resources in *myView* support my small group instruction?

The Assess and Differentiate pages in the Teacher's Edition are great resources for instruction suggestions for small groups as well as independent work.

Additional Resources

Strategy Support

- Strategy Group section of Assess and Differentiate pages in the Teacher's Edition
- Routines and anchor charts in the Small Group Guide

Differentiated Instruction

- ELL Targeted Support suggestions throughout the Teacher's Edition
- Teaching suggestions for Intervention, On-level, and Advanced Learners in the Teacher's Edition

Leveled Text

- Leveled Readers in print and digital formats
- Support for selection and using the Leveled Readers in the Teacher's Edition and Small Group Guide

Writing Development

- Writing Workshop pages in the Teacher's Edition
- Writing anchor charts in the Small Group Guide

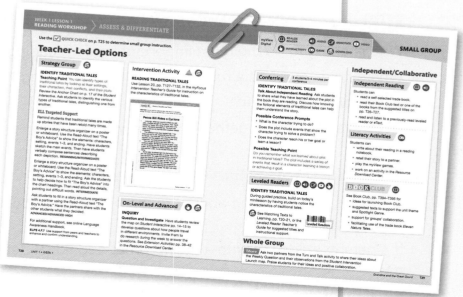

Chapter 5

Independent and Collaborative Work in Action

Questions Addressed in This Chapter

- What will the rest of the class do during small group time?
- How can I manage questions and other interruptions?
- How can I monitor the work other students are doing while I'm leading a small group?
- What resources in *myView* help me facilitate independent and collaborative work?

How can I make certain the whole class stays engaged in meaningful work?

by Ernest Morrell, Ph.D.
Professor, Wake Forest
University and Jim
Cummins (ELL), Ph.D.
Professor Emeritus,
University of Toronto

What factors lead to student engagement?

Students are more likely to be engaged in an activity if they believe that they can be successful, if they find the work relevant and appropriately challenging, and if the activity has some implicit value to them. Students are also engaged when they have the opportunity to collaborate with classmates and when they can share their work with others. As students become more conscious of the world around them, they want to be involved in activities that serve a meaningful purpose, such as informing others, entertaining others, or making some real change. They also want to embrace an identity they see as powerful or valuable, such as a writer, researcher, scientist, or lawyer.

How do students acquiring English benefit from working in collaborative groups or with partners?

Teachers can assign roles to students within the group, ensuring that roles assigned to English language learners are consistent with their current English proficiency levels and their talents and interests. For example, beginning or intermediate students might take on the role of creating visuals (drawings, charts, photos) for a project or they might use their home languages to research relevant information available on the Internet.

While they are planning and carrying out a group project with other students, English language learners will come into contact with relevant academic language and content in a social context that supports comprehension.

What are common pitfalls to avoid when planning tasks for the rest of the class?

Many contemporary dynamic literacy classrooms have students working simultaneously on different projects, some individually and others in small groups. This allows teachers to differentiate instruction, to have students collaborating in small groups, and to focus on a handful of students while others work independently. While they are sometimes logistically tricky for teachers, these classrooms offer tremendous benefits for individualized, differentiated, and small group learning. They also increase oral language fluency by giving more students an opportunity to speak in class.

Don't make group time too long for students. While all concurrent activities should be of a similar length, there can be diminishing returns if the activities run too long. Shorter is better.

The following should be used as a checklist when planning for small groups and collaborative work:

- Everyone understands what they are responsible for working on or completing.
- Students are able to work independently if the teacher needs to focus on small groups.
- Activities are of equal duration so all students feel sufficiently occupied.
- There is a good balance between quiet activities and activities that require social interaction.
- Classroom Environment
  - Everyone has an environment conducive to the work they have been asked to do.
  - Students are sufficiently spaced throughout the classroom so they do not unnecessarily bother other groups or students.
  - Active groups are huddled up so that they can do their work in a way that doesn't disturb other students.

What is a good way to introduce independent work and collaborative tasks at the beginning of the year?

A few years ago, Ms. Jackson ran into some management issues with students in her class when they weren't involved in her small group. She focused on learning some techniques that she has since shared with her teammates.

Start Small

At the beginning of the year, I focus on behavior and use of the classroom systems. My students need to know what I expect and how they can manage materials and movement. They practice filling in assignment logs and reaching consensus with and giving feedback to a partner using simple tasks that I know they can do.

Add New Tasks and Tools Slowly

As students learn how to monitor their independent time and work with a partner, I introduce new tasks like reading logs, work folders, and group work with four people. The time I spend introducing the behaviors and management processes is paid back as the year goes on.

Put More Ownership on Students

My goal is to have the students self-monitoring as much as possible. They know where materials belong, how to plan and get tasks done within a group, and how to keep track of their work in progress and their completed work. They take pride in having our class operate smoothly.

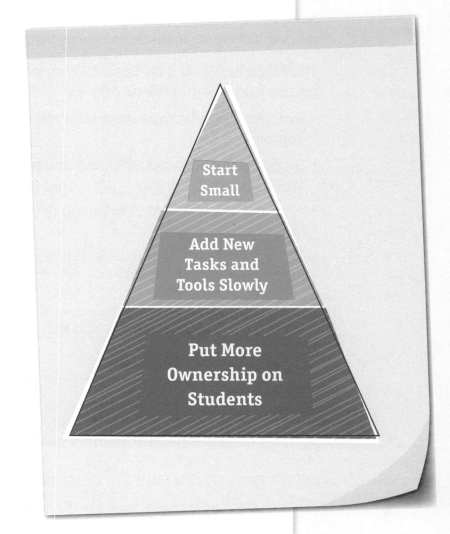

What are some ideas to address common challenges managing students who are not working in the small group?

Challenge	Ideas
How can I better manage a disruptive student who is not part of the small group I'm teaching?	• I might move the student closer to my small group area. • Using peer support might help. If the disruptive student is at a table with others, I might compliment whole tables for their quiet work.
What is a tip for lowering the noise level in the classroom without stopping my small group?	• I keep a large chart by my chair. It has a thermometer shape on it. Without saying anything, I clip clothespins on it to match the noise level. The class knows there are positive and negative consequences for the results at the end of the period.
How can I hold students more accountable for staying focused on their independent work?	• If a student isn't consistently completing the work on the assignment log by the end of the period, I break the work into smaller chunks. I check in with the student between small groups to help them learn to pace themselves better.
What can I do with my "fast finishers"?	• I have a chart listing what to do if students finish their work. I just look at the student from across the room and point to that chart as a reminder.

What should I consider when assigning independent work?

Students need to see that the work is relevant to what they are learning and that they are accountable for completing the work. They need to have clarity on how to complete the assignment, what materials will be needed, and when the assignment should be completed. If some of the work is being completed on computers, students need to know how and where to save their work. Many teachers use assignment logs to help students get and stay organized.

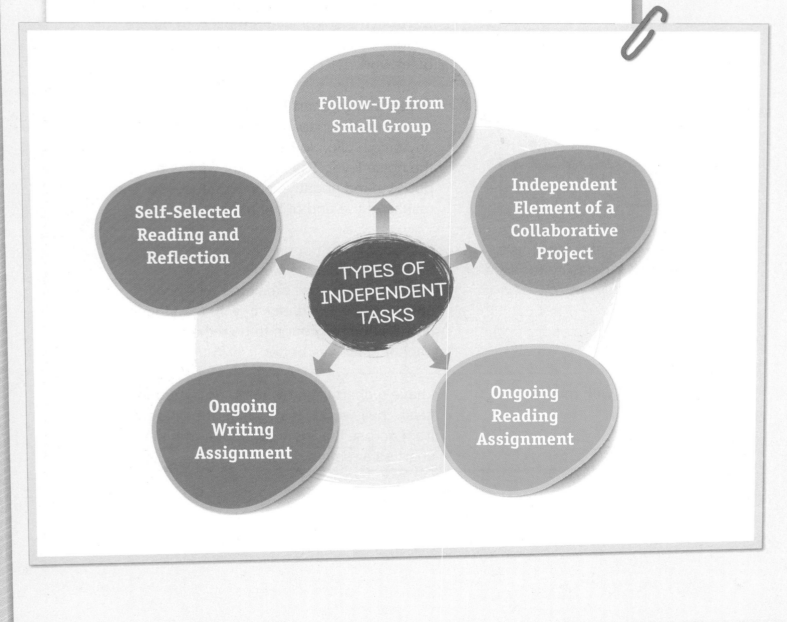

Follow-Up from Small Group

Small group lessons usually end with a follow-up activity for the students to practice and apply the teaching point. Have students restate what the assignment is and add it to their assignment logs.

Independent Element of a Collaborative Project

Collaborative projects have parts that are assigned to individuals and then put together into the larger project. This might involve research or writing that is completed outside of the collaborative group session.

Ongoing Reading Assignment

Students' academic stamina can benefit from having some tasks that are ongoing and not completed in one day. Students may be reading a book to prepare for a Book Club meeting or reading a variety of texts for a unit project.

Ongoing Writing Assignment

Just as students have ongoing reading work, they also have ongoing writing related to weekly or unit assignments. It is helpful if the assignment logs include what stage of the writing process they are working on each day.

Self-Selected Reading and Reflection

Part of being a member of a community of readers is having self-selected books to read. Include reflection activities to keep students focused and accountable.

What are some strategies that are helpful when implementing independent work?

Since students spend a good bit of the language arts time reading and writing independently, making that time count is important. Having clear assignments, checking with students during the process to note issues or confusion, and having students know that they are accountable are keys to effective independent work.

Make Assignments

How you set up the task has the most to do with how successful the task will be. If the task is new, model an example to check for questions. Before sending students to work independently, you might ask some of these questions to avoid confusion later.

- Is this like something you have done before? How is it similar? How is it different?

- What materials or supplies are you going to need? Where are they kept? What do you do with the materials when you are finished?

- Tell a partner what you will do first, second, and third.

- What could you do if you get confused or forget what to do?

- Who in this group could you ask if you have a question?

- About how long should this assignment take?

- How could this assignment be broken into smaller parts?

- What should you check when you think you have finished?

- Where does your completed work go?

Check Progress

It can prevent future problems if you have some quick ways to monitor that students are on track with their assignments.

- Have students hold up from one to five fingers to show how close they are to completing the task.

- Ask students to draw a progress bar like they see on electronic devices and color in their progress for each assignment in their assignment log. You can quickly scan the progress bars as you walk past or have students hold up their logs to show you between small groups.

- Ask students to draw three large circles on the back of their assignment logs and color them like a traffic light. Have them point to green if they feel they are making good progress, yellow if they have a question, and red if they are in great need of help. You can do a quick "traffic light check" between small groups.

Ensure Accountability

Having students know that they are accountable for their work when working independently will help them stay on task. Self-monitoring is a skill to be practiced and reinforced.

- Set up a task checklist that is visible on the work surface where the student is working. Monitor the checklist as you walk around the room.

- Break larger tasks into smaller ones for students who need to work on self-monitoring skills.

- Use an hourglass-shaped egg timer to help students establish and meet short-term goals.

- Remind students how and when their work will be assessed or shared.

- Add a self-monitoring section to the assignment log. Have students rate their focus, work, and accuracy.

How do students benefit from working with a partner?

Some students may be intimidated and cautious about speaking in a large group. Partner work provides a safe place for students to learn to express themselves and practice focused listening. Students should learn how to give useful and kind feedback, as well as accept critiques to get stronger and learn more.

Examples of Partner Work

- **Turn and Talk:** Pose a question. Let students know how long they will have to discuss it with a partner. Remind them that each person should talk and listen carefully enough to be able to retell what their partner said.

- **Think Pair Share:** Students first think about the posed question. They then share their thinking with a partner. The partners then share their ideas with another pair.

- **Mix and Mingle:** Students think about the posed question. They then circulate around the room and talk to other class members about the topic. Encourage students to take paper with them to record other ideas they hear. When partner time is complete, ask students to share some of the most interesting ideas they heard.

Rules for Working with Partners	
Review the work you need to do. Share the work.	Give each person time to talk.
Restate what your partner said to be certain you understood.	Praise and encourage each other. Disagree politely.
Make eye contact.	Speak in a voice that only your partner can hear.

When can I best use collaborative groups?

Working with others isn't just a school skill. It is a life skill. As with other skills, explicit instruction will increase the chances for success. Begin with small groups of two or three. As students' skills improve you may increase the collaborative group size to up to five or six students.

• Make it clear how the group's work will be evaluated. Many teachers assess the group's work as a whole and also each individual's contributions.

• Remind groups to end each group meeting by making certain each member knows what to do before the next group meeting.

• Involve students in self-evaluations of the group's work. Did everyone feel heard? Did everyone fulfill the expectations by completing their portion of the work? What might they do differently when they work with the next group?

Roles for Group Members

Give students opportunities to learn about some of the roles that help groups work effectively. Students should have a chance to take on all the roles during the year.

Facilitator: Keeps the group on task. Makes certain everyone contributes.

Materials Manager: Gathers, distributes, and collects materials.

Time Keeper: Monitors the schedule and lets the group know how much time is left.

Recorder: Takes notes and makes certain that members know their assignments.

Reporter: Leads the presentation of the group's work.

What are Book Clubs, and how can I set them up effectively?

Book Clubs help readers process what they are reading in a different way. When readers discuss and share opinions, they hear—and hopefully come to appreciate—that other readers may see things differently.

Choose books that give students an opportunity to develop opinions, think deeply about a theme, and enjoy talking with others about parts of the book. You may use Book Clubs as an opportunity to reinforce teaching points as you check in with each Book Club. While Book Clubs can help create better readers, writers, speakers, and listeners, there is one important thing to remember—Book Clubs should be fun!

Starting Book Clubs

There are many ways teachers can kick off Book Clubs. Here are some ideas to try.

- Hold a book preview to help students select the book they would like to read. Give a dramatic "commercial" for each book.

- Provide a variety of fiction and nonfiction titles. Book Clubs might read a fiction and nonfiction book related to the same topic.

- As students read self-selected books they enjoy, ask them to complete a nomination form on which they explain why the book might be a good choice for a Book Club.

- Ask students to suggest topics for topic-related Book Clubs. Keep the chart of the suggestions posted. As students find books that relate to the suggested topics, they can write the title next to the topic.

- When Book Club groups are formed, remind them that the group rules apply. Reinforce the idea that all members of the group don't need to share the same opinions.

Before Book Club Meetings

Students should come to Book Club meetings prepared. Make certain they know what they should read before the club meeting and have included that reading in their assignment log. Perhaps there are questions that students are asked to think about before the group meets.

Some possible questions for students to think about before discussing a book in a Book Club are:

- What have you found most interesting or surprising so far?
- What other books does this book remind you of? Why?
- What might you ask the writer to change about the book? Why?
- Do you agree with the actions of the characters? Why or why not?
- Would you like to read another book on this topic or by this author again? Why or why not?

During Book Club Meetings

As the teacher, you may not necessarily be a member of the group, but you should walk around and listen. Feel free to whisper a question or comment in a student's ear to prompt discussion of a teaching point.

Book Club Rules

Just as any club would have, a Book Club has rules. Encourage students to modify the rules as they gain more experience working as part of a collaborative discussion group.

Rules for Book Club

Come to the Book Club prepared.	Listen to what others are saying.
Ask questions to get other people's thoughts and opinions.	Support what you are saying by using examples from the book.
Do not interrupt each other.	People don't need to agree. Respect what others say and share your own ideas.

What makes a task authentic?

Seeing the value and relevance of work increases students' engagement and focus. Students are given a real-world task to apply the skills they have learned.

Characteristics of Authentic Tasks

Real World Issues

- Select a task or scenario that is familiar or relevant to students.

- Projects that result in students making a difference can be highly motivational.

Higher-Level Thinking

- The end result of the task should not be identical for each student or group. There should be decision points along the way where different paths may be selected.

- Students should be involved with evaluating information and making informed decisions that they can justify by citing specific information.

Discussion and Planning

- Authentic tasks help students apply speaking, listening, and collaboration skills.

- Breaking a task into parts and managing time are important skills.

Use of Multiple Sources

- Authentic tasks should involve examining more than one viewpoint or reference.

- Using multiple sources requires making comparisons, evaluations, judgments, and decisions.

Polished Finished Product

- The end products from an authentic task should be ready for publication or presentation.

- The final products may be shared with decision-makers or people from the community who deal with an area related to the task.

Reflection

- Students are given time to reflect on what worked well, what they learned from others, and what they might do differently next time.

- Students should be asked to reflect on what skills they applied when completing the task.

What are some common challenges with authentic tasks?

Avoid	Try Instead
Getting overwhelmed by taking sole responsibility for gathering materials	Involve your grade-level team members, media specialist, or librarian in gathering a variety of sources for students.
Immediately providing students with all the steps needed to complete the task	Encourage students to take ownership of the task. This means they may struggle a little to make a plan. That is part of learning. Don't let them get too far off track, but do let them find their own path.
Rushing or not giving enough time for quality work	Have students work in short periods at first and lengthen the time they are given to work on the authentic task as they get into more of the "heart" of it. Students need extended time to practice and polish their work.

How can I assist with authentic tasks without students becoming dependent on me?

Schedule time for individuals or groups to check in with you. Those check-in conferences may be more frequent at the beginning of the task to be certain students are focused on the important elements of the task and have the resources they need.

If a student or group seems to be depending on you too heavily, consider issuing a finite number of "help tickets" that can be redeemed for conference time with you. This may be for planning their questions more carefully and becoming more self-reliant.

How does my role as the teacher change during the different types of instruction?

Being a teacher means wearing lots of different hats. You need to be a counselor, a nurse, a detective, a coach, and many others. Let's look at three roles that you take on when it comes to gradually releasing the ownership of learning to students.

Shifting your role as the teacher also forces students to adjust to their new roles. There are times when students need to be absorbing and interacting with new information and times when they need to practice and reflect on where they are still struggling. In addition, there are times when they need work to apply what they have learned to a different context.

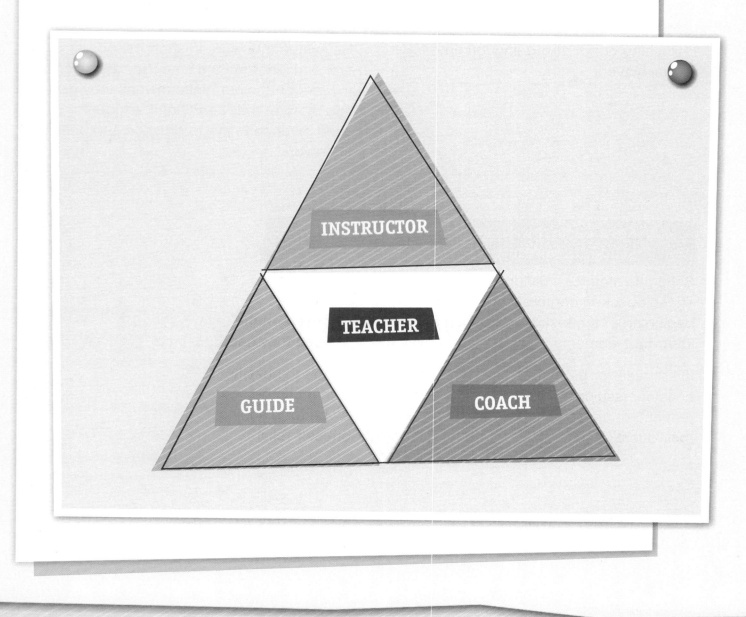

Demonstrating, modeling, and providing explicit instruction are parts of the instructor role. When instructing, the heavy lifting is being done by the teacher. This is the standard role when introducing a new teaching point in whole or small groups. Since a major objective is helping students become independent, transitioning away from being the sole instructor is essential.

A guide helps the group move forward on the right path and keeps anyone from getting lost. As a guide in the classroom, the teacher asks questions that help refocus and redirect as learners gain independence. As a guide in small group, the teacher is a reading partner who asks the questions that help the reader think more deeply about the teaching point.

Like a sports coach during a game, a coach in the classroom hands the real work to the players/learners. In coaching mode, you look for areas that deserve cheering on and areas to note for future instruction. A coach is there for questions and encouragement, but the players know it is their time to shine.

How can I help students work better independently and with others?

While we might hope that students have the social-emotional skills to work independently or work well with others, sometimes we must problem-solve to help them. Like any other skill, work habits need to be taught and practiced.

Working Independently	
If . . .	**then . . .**
students waste time gathering materials,	have students create a materials checklist. Place materials within reach in containers with compartments to keep supplies organized.
students forget the directions or assignments,	have students restate the directions. Encourage students to keep an assignment log and have partners check each other's entries when assignments are added.
students bother other learners,	have students focus for a short amount of time to learn what focusing *really* is. Gradually extend that focus time.
students rush through assignments,	provide a checklist for students to check that they have fully completed their assignments. You might try giving a minimum number of minutes per assignment to break the independent work time into chunks. provide more frequent progress check-ins. You might arrange the assignments from simplest to most complex to give the student a sense of accomplishment. Try to determine if the student is having problems with focusing.

Working as Part of a Group

If . . .	then . . .
a student becomes domineering,	consider a group recording sheet. Ask students to put a check by their name when they speak. For example, a person cannot speak again until there is a check by each person's name.
a student is shy about talking,	develop some nonverbal ways for the group to share opinions such as voting or adding sticky notes to pages or discussion charts.
the group keeps getting off-topic,	ask the group to generate a list of questions to answer or topics to discuss. Suggest that group members take turns making certain one question or topic is addressed.
members of the group become argumentative,	provide some explicit instruction on sentence starters to use when you disagree with someone. Examples include: *I heard you say ___, but I was thinking ____. That's interesting. Have you thought about ____? Can you show me what you read that made you think that?*
students are too willing to accept the first comment,	show them the value and fun of a lively discussion by teaching some conversation extenders, such as: *What might be another way to look at this? Can you tell more about why you think that? What points can be made on the other side?*
the group's work remains very basic or bland,	give students some conversation starters to add to their discussion, such as: *What might happen if ___? Another way to think about it is ___. If we had to do it differently, we could ___.*

Independent Work Anchor Charts

Partner and Group Work Anchor Charts

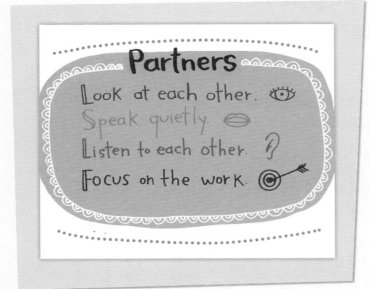

What resources in *myView* support my planning for independent and collaborative work?

Choose among these *myView* resources available to support independent work, partner work, collaborative groups, and Book Clubs.

Independent Work

- Independent Reading and Independent Writing suggestions in the Teacher's Edition
- Student Interactive pages
- Reading Log in the Student Interactive
- *myView* Games

Partner and Collaborative Group Work

- Turn, Talk, and Share suggestions in the Teacher's Edition
- Small Group pages in the Teacher's Edition
- Project-Based Inquiry ideas in the Teacher's Edition
- Writing Club suggestions in the Teacher's Edition
- Collaborative Conversations pages in the Resource Download Center on PearsonRealize.com

BOOK CLUB

- Weekly Book Club suggestions in the Teacher's Edition
- Trade books available for Book Club on PearsonRealize.com